A
PEEP
AT THE
POMS . . .

A
PEEP
AT THE
POMS ...

The Australian Captain in England

ALLAN BORDER

With Peter Bills

ARTHUR BARKER LIMITED
LONDON
A subsidiary of Weidenfeld (Publishers) Limited

I would like to express my thanks to Peter Bills, without whose help this book would never have been written.

Published in Great Britain by
Arthur Barker Limited
91 Clapham High Street
London SW4 7TA

ISBN 0 213 16946 0

Printed in Great Britain
by Butler & Tanner Limited
Frome and London

Contents

To the dressing-room boys and the staff at Chelmsford who all contribute to 'The Essex Way'.

Illustrations

1

Herbaceous Border!

My home city of Brisbane had never seemed so appealing! From 27,000 feet up somewhere above the English Channel, I couldn't see very much at all for thick cloud. But my mind was as clear as the brightest, best Brisbane summer day. Thoughts raced across my mind – and I've got to concede they weren't of English summer gardens and tea on the lawn with cucumber sandwiches. Instead, I was thinking of barbecues in the backyard, breakfast on the house veranda . . . a drive to Surfer's Paradise.

I knew what I was missing. Deep-blue skies, warm sunshine without being over hot . . . perfect days for the next five months. But more than all those things, I knew I was missing one potentially vital aspect in my career – five months of comparative rest from the rigours of playing professional cricket. You can come to terms with leaving Brisbane's climate . . . if you have to. I guess you can come to terms with six months in solitary, too! But the thought in my mind was why I was going through all this. It didn't make sense.

I had got back from Australia's long, often unsuccessful tour of New Zealand and almost fallen into the arms of my wife, Jane, at Brisbane Airport. I was tired and I knew it. I needed to forget about bats, pads, fast bowlers and especially the needs of a side. Hang it, let the cricket merry-go-round continue without me, I thought. Stop the world – I want to get off. I understood the sentiment behind that phrase.

The thought of starting all over again, in far away England in a couple of weeks' time, was making me highly sceptical. I felt mixed up, uncertain. Part of me said it was something I had always wanted: the chance to play English County cricket, particularly for a successful team like Essex: a great idea. The other half, influenced no doubt by weariness in body and mind, pleaded for rest, condemning the exercise upon which I was now embarked as at best romantic and at worst, quite inappropriate.

Of course, I had known at the end of the Australian tour the previous summer that, I was going to return to England and play for Essex. It had excited me, too, at that stage. England ... the country I had visited so often and toured several times in recent years. I seemed to know it almost as well as Australia! Like in 1981 when Ian Botham turned the entire Ashes series upside-down; and in 1984, when I had enjoyed a marvellous time in the company of Greg Chappell, playing a little cricket and plenty of golf as well as watching that thrilling sportsman Seve Ballesteros win the British Open title at St Andrews. For an Aussie to see that at first hand, as well as get the chance actually to play the famous Old Course at St Andrews, was memorable. There had been plenty of other years in England, too, going back, for instance, to 1977 when I had an enjoyable season with Gloucestershire's Second Eleven.

So what happened between leaving England in September 1985, having led the Australian touring team to defeat in the Ashes series, and April of the following year, when my plane started its descent into London's Heathrow Airport? To be blunt, an awful lot, much of it immensely disappointing and taxing from a personal viewpoint. I had played so much cricket I felt overwhelmed by the game's demands. For a start, I'd experienced the dubious privilege of leading the Australian cricket team to defeat in the series against New Zealand on our own soil, for the first time in history. I needed records of that nature like a hole in the head. To compound the disappointment, I had taken the side to New Zealand and lost the Test series there, too. Only a gutsy comeback in the one-day internationals on the other side of the Tasman – when we hauled ourselves back from a 2–0 deficit to draw the series 2–2 – had given us much cause for satisfaction. And by then, with the Test matches lost, I was in no mood for humour. We knew that the Kiwis had done the double over us. It was a hell of a record to live with, leading the Aussies to defeat at home and away against New Zealand – the nation we had become accustomed to turning over.

I remember seeing a photograph of Jane and myself at Brisbane Airport when I finally got home, via Melbourne. The joke went around that it was unclear who was holding whom up – Jane, in relief at seeing me again and having someone to help her, or myself, through exhaustion, clinging on to the person who had meant so much to me. It wasn't a bad joke, either. I felt pretty whacked and ready for a long, long rest. But somewhere in the back of my mind, nagging away like a migraine, was a date, an aircraft ticket and a journey to London. I had just two weeks to get unpacked, rested up and then packed again, plus help with all the preparations for getting two little children across the world. That is about as easy a task as plotting the assault on the Somme! I began to wonder what I had done, not only to myself but my family as well. But it was too late to change my mind at this stage.

The flight was unexceptional. As the aircraft climbed out of Brisbane, the city laid out beside the river a long way below us, the doubts started again. A short stop in Singapore, where we went for a stroll in Changi Airport's ultra-modern airport complex, took my mind off it. We stretched our legs and gave Dene, my little three-year-old boy, his first view of the Far East. Nicole, who was then just ten weeks old, slept soundly. And then, after another re-fuelling stop around the Middle East in the middle of the night, we flew on, hour merging into hour, night seemingly endless. The Greek Islands passed below us, little lights twinkling on the tiny islands with the black surround, the Aegean Sea. Only an hour or two out from London did the first streaks of daylight start to appear on the horizon. Europe lay before us and quite soon, the descent for London . . .

I have to be honest. No way did I feel: Oh great, we're nearly there and I'm so looking forward to it. Instead, the panic buttons started to be pressed. Oh God, what am I doing here, I thought to myself. I could have been lying in the sun, enjoying a few cool beers and lapping up the good weather. I thought, Is this *really* what you want to do?

My mental attitude towards cricket during the past twelve months had begun to suffer. It had become a chore. In a sense, the fact that I was coming to England to play County cricket was a new ball game, especially as I wouldn't be captain. A new bunch of blokes to play with; I was, in a sense, attracted by it. But the fact that I was so tired countered that view. I am, after all, a believer in the theory that it is perfectly possible to suffer overkill in any sport.

There was one good thing about the flight; the children got through the twenty-six hours extremely well. When you bring two small children on so long a flight, you wonder how they will handle it. But both were great, sleeping for periods so that Jane and I could do likewise, taking it in shifts to look after them. British Airways were superb, too. Airlines get their 'stick' at times, but not from me on this occasion. They put us in Super Club class and helped immensely with settling down the kids. Jane and I watched all the fuss and attention and grinned at each other; we had travelled a lot on our own and had never been as well looked after as this! And when we landed, the excellent treatment continued.

We were met by the Essex people and driven straight out to Chelmsford, to the house which was to be ours for the summer. The local manor house? Well, not exactly, but it was just what we wanted; somewhere for the children to be settled, with a back garden if the weather was good. And a home to call our own.

The weather? I'll be diplomatic and say it was cool. The pilot clearly had a sense of humour – he said London was basking in temperatures of two degrees. The sky was grey, with a light drizzle falling. Welcome to the English summer! But if the weather was enough to give you the blues, then a bloke by the name of Ray East certainly wasn't going to be inhibited in terms of losing his humour just because it was more like November than late April.

'Eastie' has a reputation as just about the funniest man around the County circuit. And it didn't take me long to realize why. We had got to the house around ten o'clock in the morning and I didn't want to go to bed. I find that with long flights across the world, the best thing to overcome jet lag is to try and stay up all day from the morning when you arrive. If you can do that and get through to about nine or ten o'clock that night, you then crash out, get a good night's sleep because you are so tired and wake up feeling right the next day. I have tried going to bed upon arrival and for me it just doesn't work. That's the theory, anyway!

So when the Essex officials asked me if I wanted to go down to the County ground to meet a few people and have a look around, I was quite keen to go along with the idea. The boys were there, practising with wickets out of doors despite the weather, and although conditions were not ideal, I figured it was useful practice. After lunch they were going out to the nets again and I thought I'd join them and have a hit. So I went out, borrowed all sorts of gear and got a bat.

4

But I started to bat like an absolute drunk. I was hitting them all over the place, then getting bowled and everything else. I wasn't striking the ball too well but I wanted to have a go, that was the main thing. But then I was bowled a couple of times and Ray East was standing at the back of the nets watching. He came out with this comment which had the lads rolling about. 'Crikey,' said Eastie, 'we've got the wrong one. We've got herbaceous border!'

Eastie is an amusing man and I can imagine playing with him would be quite a funny experience. He's a slightly madcap type character. Whenever I've seen him, he's always had a humorous story to tell about the match he's just played in or the way the umpires cocked it up, or something. Perhaps his mannerisms tend to make the story funnier than it actually is, but he is just one of those fellows who make people laugh.

There was the story of Eastie in a Second Eleven match during the season, sitting on the pavilion balcony while his team was batting. There was a telephone call for one of the Essex boys who was walking around the ground at the time. An attendant took the call and asked East where the player was. 'Over there somewhere,' said East, waving one of his arms towards the other side of the ground. Eastie hadn't settled back in his chair for more than a couple of minutes when the batsmen appeared. Eastie looked puzzled. 'Lunch time already, lads?' he queried. 'No, we've declared, haven't we?' said one. 'Wasn't that you waving to us to come in?'

A few days later, it all started in earnest, my first season in first-class County cricket in England. And I couldn't have picked a nicer place to begin than the Fenner's ground at Cambridge. The pressure was on me, even though the match was against the University. I always expect to score runs, but I wanted to do well, especially that day. It was my first game for Essex and I didn't want people looking at me and thinking, Oh hell, we've got a dud here. Fenner's is an attractive ground to play cricket on, but it's fairly open and when the wind blows, it's quite cool. When we played there with the Australians in 1985, it was a magnificent day with bright, hot sunshine. A lot of people were there and it was a really good day out. But this time conditions were bleak. An icy wind blew across the ground and everyone looked frozen. But I made some runs, 80, which was not a bad start. I felt I hit the ball reasonably well but it's always hard to tell in those conditions and against a University attack.

Cambridge always looks a super place but I've never had the time to have a really good look around. Derek Pringle lives there so I've been to his home and a couple of pubs in the area. But the way the County scene is in England, you drive in to play cricket and when you've finished, you drive out again. You never get the chance to do any sightseeing.

The next day was quite a contrast. It had rained heavily overnight and the game started half an hour late. But we could play all day under a sun. It wasn't quite as warm a sun as the Barbados variety but it would do! The game, however, wasn't as bright.

I had struggled a little for that 80 at Fenners because the wicket had a little juice in it, was slow and seamed around. Brisbane isn't like that, I have to tell you! But we got to Edgbaston in Birmingham for the match against Warwickshire and it was a really good track. I went in and was starting to hit the ball really well – 20, 30. Not bad. But when I reached 34, a new Warwickshire bowler named Tim Munton bowled me an absolute corker; you know the sort of thing . . . pitched leg, hit off, sort of ball. It was his first wicket in first class cricket. A good moment for him but a disappointment for me, because I had just started to go well. It was a bleak, overcast day and a a lot of rain was around throughout the match. But the wicket did impress me for that early stage of the season.

Brian Hardie made 81 on the second day of the match, the Sunday. I've got to be careful here so I'll say Brian has got a unique technique! It is really about the best way to describe him. He is very unorthodox in his strokeplay but highly effective in the way he manages to put his scores together. I know he is an extremely frustrating player for fast bowlers. Bowl a really good ball at him and he'll snick it through third slip region for four. Bowl him a shocker and you might get him out! Bowlers must look at him and ask: 'How can he play like this and get away with it?' Brian's secret, I'd say, is that he has a very good eye and a freakish technique which he has adapted so well.

Our second highest scorer in the innings was Derek Pringle, who made 46 not out and confirmed, for me, his great improvement. When I first saw Derek play, I thought he would really struggle to become a consistent England all-rounder. That was in Australia during 1983–84 and he was no more than a handy medium pacer without being brilliant. And he was only an average batsman. But the development from then to now has been enormous. His bowling has come on in leaps and bounds and his batting, too, has improved out of sight. The innings I have seen him play this season make him look a player of genuine international class, capable of playing for England.

At his pace Derek gets that little bit of bounce and also movement off the seam which makes him a difficult proposition. With his batting, he plays very straight and very correctly. OK, he might not get as much assistance from conditions in Australia, perhaps a point the selectors had in mind when they chose the England squad for the 1986–87 Australian tour at the end of the season. However, he is one of those players you always like to have in your side. Someone who can bowl tightly, take the odd wicket and a guy who will score runs in all sorts of situations. Derek is also a good striker of the ball if the situation demands.

The improvement, looking at Derek Pringle over the last few seasons, is incredible and you would expect that improvement graph to keep going up. His own confidence is high, too, which is a significant factor. It is amazing how much the game is played on confidence and in the mind. Slight improvements in technique and confidence can make you a hell of a lot better as a player and I think this is what has happened to Derek. He has got over his University days when you are not totally concentrating on your cricket, with other things to consider.

People made the mistake during the 1986 season of trying to make comparisons between Derek and Ian Botham, whom he replaced in the England side when 'Both' was suspended. But I felt that was totally unfair. They are both all-rounders, I suppose, but the comparison ends there in any meaningful sense. They are totally different players. Derek was picked early for England when he was still at Cambridge and, to a degree, I am in favour of that approach. Clearly, the selectors would have chosen him on potential more than anything else in those days, but I don't see that as such a bad thing. If you have the nucleus of a settled side at Test match level and all of a sudden, a young player shows that promise of being a top-class player, then obviously it's a good opportunity to bring him in there. That is the ideal situation. So if a guy shows enormous talent at eighteen, nineteen or twenty I say give him a chance and see what he can do. Sometimes it is too early but it is still a test of character for that fellow to see whether he can drop out of the scene and then make his way back after he has gone through the learning process. If he doesn't do it then it's just one of those things, but I'm a believer in the thought that if the guy does show talent whatever his age, then give him a go. The England selectors did it with Graham Gooch in 1975 because he obviously had the potential. Maybe he was thrown in a little too early but to his credit, he has worked hard at his game and now he is one of the *premier* batsmen around.

There was another interesting character for me to watch in that game with Warwickshire. Dennis Amiss made 108 and made them pretty well. And the way he made his runs reinforced my belief that he could and should have played a lot more Test cricket than he actually ended up doing. I don't know all the whys and wherefores of his selection history. He had a bad tour of Australia in 1974–75 when Dennis Lillee certainly sorted him out. From then on, he seemed to be an in and out sort of player. But anyone who has scored a hundred first-class centuries and taken 262 not out off the West Indies in a Test match at Kingston, Jamaica, makes you feel they should have played a lot more Test cricket than Dennis did. Against us, his innings was a second knock century. We were hoping for some sort of declaration or target to chase but War-wickshire were not prepared to do it and the game fizzled out into a boring draw. We didn't exactly give Dennis runs; he had to score them. But at that stage of the game, there wasn't the same intensity of competition one might expect. But having said that, he still batted very well and looked like a class player.

Frankly, we were disappointed Warwickshire didn't set us a target. We felt that in the first game of the season, they should have been prepared to gamble on winning or losing. Their excuse was that the wicket was too good and that against us and our strong batting line-up, they didn't feel they had a chance of bowling us out in, say, 60 overs with a target of around 280 to get. But what is that phrase ... 'nothing ventured, nothing gained'? I thought of that at the time.

Our lads were certainly disappointed. We wondered whether we were being penalized because we were a good side. That seemed harsh. I confess I don't understand the attitude Warwickshire took. To me, you have got to gamble to win any match unless it's a rout. Keith Fletcher's view corresponds more with mine: namely, that when you play twenty-four County games, you probably only need to win twelve of them and you'll win the Championship. So you might win twelve and lose twelve but you will still finish either at the top of the Championship or thereabouts. So I would have thought that at every opportunity a captain should try and play for a result.

The Essex boys feel that sometimes they have to set ridiculously easy targets to get sides interested in playing a match to a conclusion. But maybe that's the price you pay for being a good County with a strong line-up.

We got home from Edgbaston on Tuesday night and had a few days off. I was slightly surprised because the belief about English cricket is that you are playing all the time, seven days a week. I had only just started and was now enjoying a three-day break before the first of the one-day matches, in the Benson and Hedges Cup competition.

For that match, we had to go down to Hove on Friday night. So we negotiated the M25 traffic and the horrors of the Dartford Tunnel before reaching the M23 Brighton road, in Sussex. It doesn't take long unless you get caught in that tunnel blockage. That can be bad.

It turned out to be a curious affair against Sussex. We started late due to the weather and Sussex ended up being fined £1,000 for their slow over rate. I should think their treasurer was thrilled about that! It seemed to me that their captain, John Barclay, thought that after a late start, they would have all one day to bowl at us and we would have all another day bowling at them. He seemed to forget you have 3 hours 45 minutes to bowl your 55 overs which I think is about the right mark. In Australia, we get $3\frac{1}{2}$ hours to bowl 50 overs. I don't think that is unreasonable and most teams seem able to stay within those limitations especially when they are bowling first. You ought to be able to hustle through your overs when you bowl first. Bowling second, sometimes the game gets tighter at the end and you want to take a little more time over your field placings. That is when the time can slip away from you.

For me, limited-over games are OK as long as you have a good blend with three-day Championship cricket so that young cricketers do understand the difference in batting technique and approach. In three-day cricket, you obviously have a chance to build an innings and play correctly. I see Sundays as a chance to score your runs very quickly and in the process test out your technique. But if a young player is in the side just to play one-day cricket it has to be very difficult for him. And sometimes these days you get a young cricketer who can bat and bowl a bit, so he gets picked for the one-day games and not the three-day Championship stuff. To me, that's not right and certainly not fair. In that event, his development is not what it could be if he was given the opportunity to play the proper three-day cricket. But having said that, I've got to be honest and say that, overall, I think the system in England is a good one for young cricketers.

Against Sussex, Neil Foster bowled 11 overs for 70 runs and that might have seemed surprising coming from an England bowler. But Neil is still young and fairly inexperienced. Besides, that sort of thing can happen in one-day cricket; I would be reluctant to draw too many conclusions from figures in any one-day competition.

Perhaps Neil's problem is that although he has played a fair number of games for England, he still has not got the conditioning of bowling six 'dot' balls, all on the spot, especially in one-day cricket. He struggled in the early part of the season to put things together and against Sussex, Imran took to him because he was bowling a bad length. But like all aspects of cricket – if you are not quite in the groove, it is a difficult game. It doesn't matter what standard you reach – if you are not quite on your game, you struggle. That is why cricket is such a great leveller.

When you consider, too, the incredible injury Neil had to his back, perhaps people have expected rather too much too soon. He has a huge screw inserted and he's got a terrible scar right down his back, probably eight inches long. To return after that sort of injury and play at the level he has reached, has been some achievement, in my book. I don't think Neil has the pace to be a genuine quick bowler. So he must rely more on accuracy and movement off the wicket. At twenty-four, he still has a long way to go. Whether he can find a yard of pace from somewhere by building himself up, I don't know. It's up to him to work on.

I was struggling a bit for runs in that game. Yet I couldn't have had a better launch pad when I went in – 'Goochie' and Brian Hardie had put on 139 for the first wicket. Gooch made 73 and Hardie got 119 not out. But I couldn't make much of a fist of it. The conditions were a bit strange; it was pretty cool and I was struggling to get the middle of the bat on to the ball. It seemed to me that I ought to get out the old prayer mat and hope some good weather would turn up, pretty smartly!

That superb start put us well in charge. Our 277 for seven in 55 overs included 28 extras, the third highest score on our card. In a one-day fixture, I thought Sussex were too careless in bowling 12 wides and 7 no-balls. You can't afford to be as generous as that particularly when five runs might make the difference between winning and losing.

Sussex needed to score at a rate in excess of five an over to win, a stiff target against our attack. And although they had reached 80 for one by the close on Saturday night, they had taken 28 overs to get them, and were well behind the clock. That factor influenced the outcome on Monday.

But before that, on Sunday, we had to go back to Chelmsford for the John Player League game against Warwickshire. The chance for some revenge upon the side that wouldn't give us a target? Well, I don't believe professional cricketers work in those ways but I suppose you could say Goochie and Hardie might have been trying to prove a point when they thrashed 184 for the first wicket. Gooch made 100, Hardie 95 and, again from first wicket down, I was relieved to experience a traditional Chelmsford wicket which was true. I made 40, which included hitting Munton for 6, which was nice for me considering he had bowled me at Edgbaston. Our 284 for four was always going to be enough even though Warwickshire recovered from 52 for four to 237 for four. But we had sufficient runs in the bank from the start.

A good win – but no chance of a rest. We packed up, flung everything into the bags and headed back to Hove ready to resume the Benson and Hedges one-day game the following morning. But again, we had enough runs in hand, despite conceding a century for the second time in two days. Asif Din's 108 not out at Chelmsford had been a good innings but Imran Khan thrashed us for 112, again unbeaten, to win the Gold Award. But it couldn't help Sussex win the match, even though Imran's century came off only 84 balls. Sussex did well to reach 259 for six and we won by 18 runs. In truth, we always had it under control. Imran batted beautifully just to remind us what a genuine class all-rounder he really is.

Someone else batted fairly well, if briefly, that week to show what he was really capable of. And he surprised me greatly. Chris Tavaré only made 29 out of Kent's 272 in the first innings of the Championship match at Chelmsford. But 'Tav' interested me. He is one of those fellows who never really allowed himself to play his natural game in Test cricket. From what I can gather talking to players around the County circuit, he is quite a good stroke player when he is going, in County cricket. But he can play the dour innings I know him for. So when he puts his mind to it, he can be as good a striker of the ball as anyone around. But I have never seen him play that flowing cricket; it's always been the long, snail-like innings in Tests. I feel sure that probably hindered his Test career because he allowed himself to get too bogged down. He didn't play naturally, although every time I played against him, he did a bloody good job for England. But playing that way was to the detriment of his own career.

The match against Kent showed us a sight of Graham Dilley in his comeback season. And he looked impressive, bowling extremely quickly against us and looking from that moment on, as though he was going to play for England all season.

Graham had cut down his run and looked better for it. I think he has a great affinity with John Lever who was with him in Natal last year and helped him to cut down his run-up. The potential is still there for Graham to become England's *premier* strike bowler for several years to come. He is quick, intelligent and can cause problems to the best. He moves the ball away from the right-hander.

I know that some people have said Graham Dilley's action isn't that great at the delivery stride and he doesn't get his body into it enough. They say it's only an arm action at the end – and maybe it is. But if you want to analyse bowlers that closely, you would say a fellow like the former Australian Test bowler Max Walker would never have been allowed to bowl, with his action. And remember Mike Proctor – he had a terrible action, but the final result was what counted. I think that is the same with Graham Dilley. He should forget what people say about changing his action. Stick to it if you get wickets, that's the motto people like Max and Mike would proclaim. And I would tend to agree with them. As long as Graham Dilley has pace and moves the ball around, which he does, then he will have success. I don't believe it's a good idea to get too wrapped up in techniques. For me, the textbook shows you a certain amount of things but it is your own natural way of doing it that really matters. What a player should try and achieve is maximum efficiency from what God gave him. If you bat or bowl a certain way, make sure you get the maximum benefit from that style.

I believe Dilley got too tied up with being technically correct and I don't think that is the answer. As soon as you start running in and you want to bowl like Dennis Lillee, Jeff Thomson or Fred Trueman, you change completely. And that's a mistake some cricket coaches are guilty of; persuading young players to adopt another style, alien to their own natural way. The coaches seem to want everyone to be stereotyped but I don't believe that is the idea of sport. Everyone has their own little idiosyncrasies and their own way of doing things. The textbook should be there as a guide, no more.

From afar and close at hand, I have watched Dilley's career over the last few years. He impressed me when he was first in Australia. He had a lot of get up and go, possessed genuine pace and showed a lot of guts with the bat. But his batting has certainly gone backwards since then. In 1981, when he made 50 to help Botham turn around that Ashes match at Headingley, he looked to me as though he could develop into a healthy all-rounder. He seems to have let his batting slip in favour of trying to get himself fit and his bowling right. Now those two elements of his play seem right, perhaps his batting will come back in due course.

Graham is fairly tall and looks as though he can go all day. So with those attributes he ought to be in there for years assuming he stays free from injury. Whether his County captain, Chris Cowdrey, can join him in the England Test side, I'm not so sure. I find him one of those difficult players to analyse properly. He doesn't always look as though he's going to produce an innings and when he is bowling, he often looks innocuous. But he's one of those fellows who seems to nip in and take his two or three wickets and get his occasional 60 or 70 runs. And yet if he could just become a little bit better at one or the other, he could probably play for England again. He is a great fielder, but I don't think he considers himself an all-rounder; more a captain and middle-order batsman and the bowling is just a bit of a sideline. But he does produce the unplayable ball, now and then. Overall, I'd say he probably needs to become a slightly better batsman or bowler with the other complementing it, to play for England again.

Graham Dilley certainly looked a Test match bowler against us. He did the hat-trick and bowled very well. Kent went on to beat us, deservedly so, too, because they played some very good cricket. I remember the Chelmsford wicket had a fair amount of bounce for that game and Dilley looked menacing at times. The Chelmsford wicket has also acquired more pace now than used to be the case. So against Kent, the medium pacers and quicker bowlers were the ones most difficult to play.

I couldn't make much of Dilley – he had me lbw for only 14.

And although Goochie stuck it out well for 60, we were 98 short of them on first innings and Chris Cowdrey gave us a stiff target by making a good unbeaten 70 in the second knock. We fell 25 runs short of the 269 we needed to win, with my old Aussie mate Terry Alderman doing the damage with five for 46 off 17 overs. Terry got Gooch, Hardie, myself, Prichard and Pringle . . . some decent scalps in that lot. Terry's bowling confirmed for me my opinion the previous summer, that our Ashes campaign had been severely dented before it started by Terry's absence.

The Australian team missed him more than any other bowler over here in that series. Terry is a proven good bowler in English conditions and the way we played and bowled and the way the series developed, it would have been very handy to have him. I know he would have taken 30 wickets plus, in the series. There were others we missed; Kim Hughes for his experience, Graham Yallop for his experience and batting ability. When he is playing well there is no better player. Carl Rackemann wasn't in the original party which seems quite strange considering what he did in South Africa. He returned to Australia from that tour with an incredible reputation but when the squad for England had been picked, he wasn't in it. But he proved in South Africa he will be a great acquisition for the future of Australian cricket. Steve Smith was another one and they should both have a lot of years ahead of them in Australian cricket. But above all those, I'd say Terry Alderman was our biggest loss. We never replaced Terry because there wasn't anyone of his kind to operate so successfully over here, and keep plugging away hour after hour.

Defeat in that Championship match wasn't the ideal tonic for the long drive to Taunton on Friday night. We faced Somerset there on the Saturday, in the next Benson and Hedges one-day game. Except, like the Sussex match, this one was also fated to drag on into the Monday. That, I found to be frustrating, especially if you had a John Player League game somewhere else on the Sunday in between. It made so much more driving.

There is no way you can face a side containing Richards, Botham and Garner without some thought of what could happen if the three of them – or even just one – breaks loose with bat or ball. But on this particular Taunton wicket, there wasn't much danger of the bat ruling the ball.

Essex made 206, going in first, but were on skid pan alley until Derek Pringle made a good 50. Then Stuart Turner went in and bludgeoned a mighty useful 41 just when we looked like struggling to make 150. That would have been too few. So we got past 200 and had a chance if we could control Richards and Botham. Akin to saying England of the 1930s and 1940s would beat Australia if they could get out Bradman! Some barrier. Richards we dismissed fairly cheaply but the game went into the second day because of bad light.

Joel Garner's figures had been one for 48 off 11 overs; by his high standards of one-day cricket, pretty expensive. He didn't go for many early on but Derek Pringle got after him at the end. We finished up knocking Joel for about 30 off his last four or five overs which is a rare pleasure for batsmen these days! But that happens even to the best bowler in one-day cricket – it is part of the game. With Joel, it is not just his height which makes him difficult; he is also a very fine bowler and moves it both ways. He has good pace to go with the height so if you combine all those qualities, he is a very difficult proposition. There are moments when he is as quick as anyone around, Marshall and Holding included.

In the West Indies a couple of years ago, Joel Garner bowled really quickly and was an awful handful. I can still feel the bruising occasionally! He got a lot of wickets against us on that tour. You head for the back foot all the time against Joel because of his extraordinary height. The ball bounces probably a foot higher than from someone of normal height. That becomes pretty difficult to combat if he gets any assistance from the wicket. It's not too bad on a normal batting track but if there is anything there, he will be more awkward than most. He is a marvellous bowler anyway but he possesses a particularly good yorker, one of the best in the business.

It was Colin Dredge, not Garner, who got most wickets that day. Numbers 2, 3, 4 and 5 in our batting line-up, too! He came on after the initial burst, when we were trying to increase the run rate. Colin bowled pretty tidily and well and he's a useful performer. But on another day, Joel might take six wickets and Colin, none. That's the uncertainty of one-day cricket – you never know what to expect from it.

I find one-day statistics, in terms of batting or bowling achieve-ments, a great distortion. You can get a guy coming on to bowl after 25 overs and because the side might have been pinned down by excellent bowling early in the innings – and intent only on survival – there is a need to improve the run rate. So a guy who starts bowling as the batsmen are looking to hit most things, might pick up four or five wickets. That's because batsmen have played strokes they would not have attempted early on. So the bowler at the start who bowled beautifully, might have beaten the bat but not got wickets, ends up with no reward. And the other guy has got quite a few without bowling anywhere near as well. Figures really mean nothing in that sort of cricket.

I started off all right that day, hitting the first few balls well enough to make me think I was going to have a reasonable chance. But then I clipped one straight behind square, right to Viv Richards. I couldn't have picked a worse bloke to give a catch to – he will never drop them. But we all struggled early on and it was only Pringle and Turner who gave us a reasonable score.

Stuart Turner might be a veteran but he's still a very useful one-day cricketer. He can smack the ball around and is just the bloke to bowl tightly in the middle of an innings because he doesn't give much away. At Taunton, that time, after making 41, he bowled 11 overs and took three for 43, which was a tremendous performance. Only near the end of his spell, at the hands of Botham, did he go for many runs. He's a super competitive guy; a good, honest player.

Somerset hadn't slept too well that night, I shouldn't think! They were 75–6, so we knew it was in the bag unless 'Both' went mad on the Monday. He did make 41 but once he went, that was it. That gave us two victories in the Benson and Hedges and we were almost through after that. We needed one more victory to make sure and we got it against Gloucestershire at Chelmsford. We made 271 for seven of which Pringle got 56 not out, Prichard 52, Gooch 51 and myself 31. It was the same story for me and I began to feel slightly concerned. I had my moments and my problems. It was, however, a scratchy performance overall and I wasn't happy. I wasn't batting well and I had to be concerned. The lads didn't say anything; they probably sensed I wasn't satisfied in myself. But cricket is cricket and anything can happen on the next day. So I felt I ought to wait a week or two before reaching for the aspirin bottle!

Gloucestershire had a tough challenge to match our score. I thought they did well to make 254 for nine. And when they reached 181–2 with Kevin Curran and Bill Athey going well, they had a good chance. But a middle-order collapse ended their chances and they got further and further behind the required run rate.

It was good to watch Athey in action again. He made 78 runs

before being run out and made them well. He's been around for a long, long time and, from what I am told, he didn't really fit in with the Yorkshire way. But he seems to have had three good years at Gloucestershire. He certainly looks a good enough player to play Test cricket on a regular basis. It has probably been a matter of the opportunity coming along ... and Bill taking it. Now, with his extra experience, I think he will become a success in Test cricket. At twenty-eight, he has the know-how to go with the technique and temperament.

Playing for your country contains an awful lot of luck, even before you walk out to bat or bowl. If you string together a couple of scores at the right time, you get picked. You might, on the other hand, play well when England are playing well and you don't get a look in. A few scores at the right time can mean the difference between playing for your country or not. That's the crazy situation with selection; sometimes it gets down to who does what at the right time.

We also ran across another interesting character in that Gloucestershire match. David Lawrence; big, strong, very energetic and powerful. You certainly cannot fault him on the fact that he gives 100% and keeps rushing in and wanting to get people out. He is incredibly enthusiastic but I would like to see him try and refine his run-up and deliveries and channel his energies a little bit better. I'm not preaching for him to get more into a textbook style but at the moment he is charging up to the wicket like a bull at a gate and just letting it go. There is nothing wrong with bowling fast and wanting to get as much speed generated as possible but I wonder what his thought process is. I suspect he is just trying to sling it down as fast as he can without really trying to analyse what he should be doing.

Perhaps David needs to sort out his attitude, however, to what it takes to get people out over an extended period. He needs to learn other arts of the fast bowler's make-up; the movement of the ball, the art of psychology and how to 'think out' a batsman. Bowling fast is fine but sheer pace, unless it is phenomenal, isn't like to get top-class batsmen out. Because if a bowler is rushing in and slinging it down without getting any movement, you can stand there and either watch the ball go by or play at it, safe in the knowledge that it isn't going to deviate at all. And deviation, movement, either through the air or off the seam, is what makes the great bowlers. They may not need pounding pace but they

17

get wicket after wicket because they create movement. And that always adds a slight doubt in the batsmen's minds.

David might enjoy playing on the bouncier wickets of Australia because he would get more response and be more difficult. But in England, with your wickets prone to softness unless it is a warm summer, he won't be as effective through sheer pace.

In Australia, we found a guy like David Lawrence. His name was Craig McDermott. He showed huge promise for years and years; he played in all the under-age groups, Under-14s, Under-16s and up. He played in the Under-19 Australian team over here a few years ago, so he was always one of these kids who was going to make it. But he first got into the Queensland side when he was about eighteen or nineteen, towards the end of Greg Chappell's reign so he got a fair amount of help from Greg. He would have told Craig that he had to learn about moving the ball, either way if possible. That was one of Dennis Lillee's greatest skills. So even when Dennis bowled off a reduced run or cut his pace a little later in his career, he was just as difficult to play because he moved the ball.

Craig played his first half-season and ended up playing in the Sheffield Shield final. It was against Western Australia, in Perth, and Dennis Lillee was in the Western Australian team. Craig sought out Dennis for advice after that match and they have been constant companions, mentor and bowler, for the last few years. And that sort of opportunity is there for most of the young cricketers in Australia. It is what a young player needs, too. In Australia, if you do want to seek out help and advice there is always a good cricketer around that you can go and see. Dennis Lillee himself used to see Ray Lindwall a lot, and I used to ask guys like Greg and Ian Chappell for advice. That education is readily available to young players at home and I would hope David Lawrence, if he really wanted to, could seek out people like Bob Willis or Michael Holding or anyone like that around the County circuit. Certainly, these young guys have got the world at their feet if they want to work hard at it.

From what I can tell, David Lawrence certainly does have the right ambition and from what I have seen, the young players do practise and play pretty hard. But you haven't got the ideal climate for outdoor nets and situations where young players can get together in the nets and practise their skills there. You have the indoor nets here but they really are not the same. In Australia, a

young fellow can always go to some outdoor nets and have a bat
or bowl. And, to my way of thinking, that makes a big difference.
If you are going to play cricket on turf, the more practice you can
get on that type of surface, the better.

David ought to be learning things from bowling in the same
County side as Courtney Walsh, the West Indian fast bowler.
Courtney bowled 11 overs, two for 65 in the match against us, but
he has clearly benefited from playing in the West Indies team that
is on top of the world at the moment and playing with the other
great players. But when you take him out of that situation and
make him the No. 1 strike bowler, he comes back to the field, so
to speak. He is still a very capable bowler with his size and he has
also got great prospects because he is only twenty-four. But he is
not yet as good a bowler as the other three in the West Indies line-
up, although he's obviously a good fellow to fall back on for future
reserves. He has an awkward action and lacks the same pace as the
other blokes in the West Indies team. But he does have huge
promise for the future because he angles the ball in at the right-
hander and can move it away off the seam.

Gloucestershire on the Tuesday at Chelmsford. Glamorgan on
the same ground, forty-eight hours later. The Benson and Hedges
programme starts to get fairly hectic so early in the season. But
with three wins from our first three games, there wasn't much
pressure on us and I suppose the fact that Glamorgan were our
next opponents, not a County regarded as the strongest on the
circuit, removed any remaining pressure. Glamorgan went in first
and struggled to 17 without loss, after 10 overs. That sort of start
is all right but it puts a lot more pressure on the fellows coming in
behind to strike a good run rate, virtually the minute they get to
the wicket. By the halfway stage they had only reached 66 for
three and our tight bowling had done the first part of its job.
Glamorgan made 205 mainly because Rodney Ontong hit 58 not
out. They struck me as a battling sort of side, good in team spirit
if slightly weak in all round talent and strength.

The Chelmsford wicket had a little bit of turn in it, and John
Steele caused us a few problems, notably when he dismissed Brian
Hardie, Paul Prichard and myself for a personal cost of just 14
runs. I had played another fairly ordinary sort of innings, which
worried me again. I got out to a little chip shot into mid-wicket,
caught by Geoff Holmes for 17. It was symptomatic of my tentative
approach, or increasingly tentative play, if you like. I wasn't sure

about the shot; I got out. And it wasn't the first time that had happened; this was really a continuation of my problems. I had not been batting well up to that point, not the sort of form I would say I was happy with. Against Gloucestershire, I had got 30 but wasn't all that convincing. Down at Sussex, I had batted badly, too. All through this early period, of the first three weeks, I had not played really well at all. Slow wickets didn't help but I wasn't in the business of making excuses. Of course, the inevitable started to happen. In one-day cricket especially, I found that every time I chanced my arm a little, I got out. It can happen but it's mighty frustrating when it does.

One guy who wasn't in frustrating form and getting out very easily, was Derek Pringle. Keith Fletcher was another. Pringle made an unbeaten 54 and 'Fletch' was not out 51 when they took us past the Glamorgan total, at 206 for four. 'Fletch' had made 42 against Gloucestershire, too. It's amazing with 'Fletch' because until this season I had only really seen him play in the 1974–75 season in Australia when the MCC got absolutely blitzed by Lillee and Thomson. My opinion of him was that he had been a good County cricket player who had struggled in that season in Australia. I didn't think he was anything fantastic. But once I met the man and came to understand how he ticks, I found him to be tremendous; a really deep thinker about the game, an excellent captain who holds an incredible amount of respect throughout Essex and I think elsewhere in England – and a mighty useful batsman, too. Watching him bat at the age of 42 against some pretty good bowling around the country, he still cut it with the best of them. So my first impressions probably were not that fair. Now I have come to understand there is a lot more to his character than I thought. His Test career had a bit of a sad end with his being dropped after losing that series to India 1–0. That was a shame and probably a loss for English Test cricket. Even in the 1986 season, when he took over from Gooch as captain when Goochie was away at the Test matches, 'Fletch' looked as good a captain as I have seen around on the County circuit. He is shrewd in the extreme, positive at all times and a man who can get the best out of his players. You only have to look at Essex's record in recent years to realize that. England lost a lot when they got rid of him.

Friday was our day off – a lie in ... what riches! And the chance to catch up with the progress of Dene and Nicole, our two youngsters. Dene is walking and into everything! So instead of watching the cricket ball intensely, I watch him pretty closely as he walks around the house. He is, it goes without saying really, a source of constant joy.

The lads should have played on Saturday ... but the English climate decreed otherwise. And then on the following day, after sitting and watching the rain fall at Northampton, at the start of a Championship match, we drove down to Gloucestershire for a John Player League game.

Gloucestershire (again) at Swindon – not the sort of match, you might think, to stir the emotions. But for me it had a special meaning because of the season I had spent with Gloucestershire, in 1977. I knew a few of their players who are still with them, so it was good to be back in their neck of the woods, talking about old times.

People might think it is hard to motivate yourself for this kind of game but I wasn't thinking of that. There were a lot of people in the ground so it was not hard to extract some excitement from it. But the wicket was very slow and wet and not really conducive to good cricket.

Unorthodox Brian Hardie again produced an innings out of nothing after Gloucestershire had batted first and made 126 for seven in 25 overs. The weather had curtailed the match to that over restriction. Brian made 71 not out and although you expect Goochie to smash it all over the place (which he did, too, for 43) Brian kept pace with him and ended up hitting the winning run. Brian is a very valuable cricketer, even though he sometimes gets out to horrendous shots. But in between, he builds really useful innings. You would have to say the textbook has gone right out of the window as far as Brian is concerned. But if he continues to make runs as he does, who is too concerned?

My own contribution was 12 not out that day but I still wasn't happy with the way I was hitting the ball. Yet one thing encouraged me. Lean spells end just as suddenly and for as slender a reason as they start. You wake up one day, have a bit of luck and you are away heading for a decent score. That is the one thought you keep in your mind amid bad spells like mine. You become the eternal optimist, the arch hope-merchant. You believe luck may turn around for you in this particular match, this week or in this setting – because you have to. You cannot lose hope. If that goes, you lose the lot.

And even when you feel you might have cracked it, events

conspire against you. Like in the Championship match against Northamptonshire. We went in late on the second day and lost Gooch and Hardie in quick succession. Northants 244 all out; Essex 5 for two when I went in to join Paul Prichard. Hardly a propitious start. And yet I started to whack the ball around and felt in better nick. Was this the change? I didn't know. I made 14 before the close in 23 for two. But if I expected the next day to bring bright sunshine into my cricketing life, I was sadly deluding myself. It rained – and it kept on raining. It washed out the rest of the Northamptonshire match and the first day of the Yorkshire game at Chelmsford, which started on the Wednesday, 21 May.

It was one month since I had started my first-class County career with Essex. But so far my best form had been as elusive as a warm English summer's day.

2

Haunted by Hadlee

Essex 295 all out. A. R. Border bowled Jarvis 1. As the second month of my season unfolded, another chance, yet another failure.

'Border was not at his best in the early season damp and was the first victim of the pitch, his off stump being wrenched out,' wrote one correspondent. But could I really blame the wicket when Brian Hardie had made 110, Paul Prichard 82 – and we had almost reached 300? Frankly, I doubted it.

Paul Jarvis bowled me with a good ball, at least I thought it was. It left me off the seam and knocked out my off pole. But I should have got some sort of contact on it ... bat, pad, whatever. If I had been in really good form, that is what would have happened. But with my feet not moving very well at the time, he got through me pretty easily, which disappointed me. I didn't want anyone thinking I was simple to knock over. But it was starting to look that way. I didn't get a chance to settle in against Yorkshire. But Hardie and Prichard batted very well, because the wicket had a bit of seam in it. They both showed you could get in on it and stay there to make runs.

At the end of the second day, Kevin Sharp and Martyn Moxon had demonstrated the same point, both with unbeaten 25s. And with the first day washed out, Yorkshire declared at their overnight 51 and we got the 'gimme' of five overs in which we scored 34, leaving them a target of 279 to win in 70 overs.

Sharp and Moxon had looked impressive on the second evening. They play nice and straight and hit the loose ball firmly. They seem to have all the right attributes. They get on with the job

23

when they get a chance to and both looked like class players to me. Again, with regard to Test appearances, it would be a question of them getting through the quagmire and being Johnny-on-the-spot when it counts. If they put together some big scores at the right time, they are probably another two players who could do well for England. Their technique and attitude are certainly correct.

The odd situation in England is that apart from an obvious couple of players, you could pick two or possibly three teams that could play a Test series against each other and you wouldn't know which side would win. There are a lot of players round about the same standard and they just need the right set of circumstances to see them get into the Test side. Only players like Gower, Gatting, Botham and Dilley stand out as obvious choices; Gooch, too. But of the others, most would acquit themselves equally as well as each other. I believe the standard is high in England. So it is always hard for a selector to get the right gel in a side. And you do need a good balance, the correct fusion of players who will go out and perform well as a unit. But in England it is very hard to know exactly what the right balance is.

When Yorkshire started their run chase, Sharp and Moxon were both back in the pavilion for only eight runs between them. At 10 for three, with Jimmy Love also gone, we were in the box seat. I thought our captain, Graham Gooch, had worked out his sums just about perfectly for the declaration. It was a good target because it gave interest to both sides and offered the white rose county the chance to attack. We had time to bowl them out and they certainly had a reasonable enough target in terms of scoring rate to make 279 very possible.

As 10 for three became 71 for three, slight furrows appeared in the old foreheads among Essex men! Those lines of concern had disappeared not long after, however, with the scoreboard reading 120 for eight. The match was ours, surely. There seemed to be no way we could fail to win with plenty more time to take the wickets of two tail-enders. But, as I was to discover twice within the next few days, true Yorkshire grit is something not to be under-estimated.

Paul Jarvis came in to join Peter Hartley and started whacking us around all over the place. When they came together, 279 looked impossible from the depths of 120 for eight. But not as they got better and better. At 244 for eight we were looking desperately for the breakthrough. It came when Pringle bowled Jarvis for 47, and although Hartley finished 87 not out, we had them out for 252 to win by 26 runs. Pringle took seven for 46 in a very good spell of bowling. The pitch had that little bit of bounce and seam in it, but those two Yorkshire players proved attack was the best form of defence. They really did play well.

If that victory was hard work, there was more of the same thirty-six hours later when we had to prepare for another match against Yorkshire – this time at Sheffield. Having finished the game at Chelmsford on the Friday night, it wasn't the ideal follow-up to have to go all the way up to Sheffield to play Yorkshire in the John Player League, especially as we didn't have a Championship game anywhere on the Saturday. The travel is the unacceptable part of the County circuit. It makes sense if you are in Taunton or Chelmsford playing a match, to have the Sunday game in the same place. But when you have to make a round trip of several hundred miles just for the Sunday afternoon match, it starts to become sheer hard work. What went on in that match didn't send us happily on the way back down the motorway on Sunday evening, either.

The match turned out to be a carbon copy of the game we had seen between Somerset and Middlesex at Taunton exactly two weeks earlier. On that occasion, because our one-day Benson and Hedges Cup match had not finished on the Saturday evening, we stayed down in Somerset for the weekend. It was too far to drive back on Saturday night and rush back down again just twenty-four hours later, ready for the resumption on Monday morning. So the lads stayed there and, with not very much to do, most of us turned up at the ground to see the Sunday game.

Somerset should have won that match easily but it ended up with them needing 15 runs off the last over. Botham was still in but with Wayne Daniel bowling, Somerset's chances didn't look too bright. When it came down to it, they got only three off the first three balls of Daniel's last over. So they wanted 12 off the last three balls of the match. Both hit a six off the fourth ball, swung mightily at the fifth but missed completely and then, with the place in pandemonium, Daniel bowled a waist high full toss at Both for the last ball and he smote it out of the ground to win the game. I had never seen anything like that before and it was great.

Anyway, two weeks later we found ourselves at Sheffield against Yorkshire. We went in first and got a pretty mediocre total – 162 all out in exactly 40 overs. However, the wicket was a slow seamer and making runs on it was very difficult. Stuart Turner again knocked it around for us at the death, making 24. Together with Keith Pont's 34, those two scores were the backbone of our innings. I went in third, with Gooch not playing, and Prichard moved up to open. I got four, bowled by Arnie Sidebottom. It did nothing to improve my mood.

When Yorkshire went in, they crashed from 70 for one, and apparent victory, to 102 for eight, and almost certain defeat. They looked stuffed out of sight. But then Paul Jarvis came in again, joining Arnie Sidebottom, and what had occurred at Chelmsford started to happen all over again. They started to hit us all around the ground and got the target down to 12 off the final over. Off the fifth and sixth balls, 10 runs were still needed and when Foster bowled the fifth, Sidebottom jumped outside his leg stump to make room for a hit outside the off. Foster bowled it just outside the off stump and was called for a wide. There were all sorts of protestations going on at that decision – we couldn't see it was fair in any way. I know there are always ifs and buts about cricket matches, but this ball was so obviously not a wide. It must have been a foot outside off stump and in normal batting conditions, that is never a wide. It was just that the batsman chose to station himself right outside leg stump and have a thrash.

The upshot was that Foster had to bowl the last two balls again. In other words, if that ball had been called good instead of wide, we would have won because Yorkshire would have wanted 10 off the last ball. As it was, Sidebottom hit the fifth ball for a boundary and then crashed the last ball over the top for six. So twice within a couple of weeks, I had seen a six hit off the last ball of the fortieth over to win a one-day match.

Of course, the Yorkshire crowd was going absolutely bananas, but I can tell you, the mood in our dressing room was not all that special, to put it mildly. It was a long drive up from Essex to lose off the last ball under controversial circumstances. It became a morbid trip back down the motorway. There were heaps of discussions afterwards about whether it was a wide, and where you should bowl a ball in those circumstances. But the simple fact was, we had lost – the rest was history. It put an end to a remarkable run of sixteen victories in succession for Essex in one-day cricket.

The Sunday League has an obvious and sizeable following in England. With spectators it clearly has a genuine place in the cricketing calendar. But in my view, it is a game purely and solely for the spectators and sponsors, not the players. If you could possibly call it something else other than cricket, you would.

To me, it is not what cricket was designed for. But it has become an offshoot of the game which is very exciting for people to watch. It is hard to play but in real terms you have just got to adapt yourself. But I am a purist and I much prefer the longer form of the game, and the tactics involved. Furthermore, I suspect basic skills have been compromised in the stampede towards more one-day cricket. It is difficult to expect players to forget the kind of strokes they have had to play on a Sunday, when they go out to bat in a Championship game on a Monday or Tuesday. Maybe it has retarded the progress rate of young players.

As a realist, however, I do appreciate the need for the shorter version of the game. But 40 overs is about as short as you want to get for a one-day game. In my opinion, the ideal length is 50 overs. I believe 60 overs is too long, the game is far too drawn out, and 55 overs is a bit messy.

As for the Sunday games, they are OK within their own context. But I would hate to be in a situation where a game got down to that 10-over slog which sometimes occurs because of weather problems. I believe that is messing about with cricket's traditional skills and tactics just too much. But if that is what has to happen, I, like everyone else, have to accept it.

I find it a bit sad that the shortened version game has basically become the lifeblood of the proper, three-day Championship stuff. You can see that any week. When Essex played Nottinghamshire at Chelmsford on a Saturday, the crowd was reasonable but no more. Yet Nottinghamshire have several star names: Robinson, Randall, Hadlee, Rice, Broad and Hemmings, plus Bruce French. All Test match cricketers. But for the Sunday game, the place was packed. So it is pretty obvious people want that sort of cricket.

As a player, I can adapt to the two forms of the game but I make a point of never looking at my averages in one-day cricket. The only thing I want to be remembered by is what I did in first-class and international cricket. I will always look back on one-day cricket as a game which can be intensely exciting. But the bottom line is, I always prefer first-class cricket.

Accepting the general fact that limited-over cricket has to have a place in the programme because of finances, I believe the English authorities have the balance about right at the moment. You would not want any more or any less cricket. I know that in Australia, we do play too much one-day cricket at the international level. Perhaps the way around the problem in my own country is to increase the amount of one-day domestic cricket.

The situation has become absurd in international cricket. We play ten lead-up games before a best-of-three final series. To me, that is far too much. You are in danger of killing the golden goose. At the moment one-day internationals are still very popular, maybe because recently the Australian team has done well, making the finals on every occasion except one. Whatever the reason, the interest in Australia is still fantastic. We played India and New Zealand last year, both supposedly unfashionable sides, compared to England and the West Indies. Yet we had record crowds watching. People just love to go to these games, especially the day–night ones. So you can imagine what it's like when England and the West Indies arrive. In the mid 1980s the interest is on the increase as far as one-day cricket is concerned and a little on the decline in terms of Test match cricket. I accept that if the one-day stuff is successful you must have it, because players expect to make a living out of the game and that is where the money is being generated. But I've got to concede I'm an enthusiastic advocate of traditional Test cricket. The instant cricket has a place but for me, not the same one as the Tests.

On the subject of crowds, Yorkshire supporters pride themselves on their knowledge of cricket, and until recent times I would have agreed with that. But the turmoil the County found itself in over the Geoff Boycott issue, staggered me. I couldn't understand why so many people believed one man was the lifeblood of Yorkshire cricket.

For an outsider looking in, it seemed that Boycott had an incredible following up there. And let's face it, the guy has been a great cricketer. But from my understandings of his interpretations of how the game should be played, it seemed to me that Yorkshire would never ever do well while he was involved with the County. Maybe as an administrator; that is one thing. But on the playing side, he was too self-motivated. Basically, Geoff only played cricket for himself. I believe Yorkshire should have said to Geoff some time ago, 'Thanks for your loyalty and service, mate, but it is time to look ahead and give the youngsters a go.'

I can't say I was surprised, therefore, by the decision at the end of the 1986 season to get rid of Boycott. The only criticism I would make is that Yorkshire should have done it years ago. It seemed they left it so long before making a decision which was best for the County and not best for Geoff Boycott.

Nobody can take away from Geoff his incredible record over the years and I would not dream of trying to do so. The man was a phenomenal scoring machine. But surely the word here should be 'was'. He has had a good run and he ought to have known it was time to go.

People who disagree will point to the fact that Geoff still scores a lot of runs. But if they say that and nothing else, they delude themselves because the fact is, he takes a lot longer to score them nowadays and that's crucially important. You might play in a match and score 120 and think you have done your job. People outside the game might think that, too. But it could also be that the guy who goes in and hits a quick 30 in a certain situation which demands fast runs, has contributed far more to the overall success of the side. Boycott has been a great player but all good things have to come to an end.

Yorkshire should produce a very good cricket side because they have got strong League cricket and an incredibly good following. So there is no excuse for them not to be doing better than they have done, over the past twenty years.

Boycott played the same way for England – that is, just for himself. But as an England Test cricketer, you can cope with that sort of situation. Having an individual bloke there just to score runs for himself isn't so bad in Tests because there is more time involved and you need someone to make big scores, anyway. But the County scene is very different. You could put up with his single-mindedness in international cricket because he was such a great player who really played well for England. That's because of the nature of the game; you can build something around someone like that. But at County level you need a certain amount of give and take and occasionally you must throw caution to the wind when you are batting. But it wasn't in Geoff's character to do that whatever the situation. So the side must have suffered.

I must say that whenever I have talked to 'Boycs' I have always got on well with him and found him quite interesting. He is good to talk to, and you won't find a more dedicated cricketer around. Yet he ought to have been a great captain and in my opinion he wasn't. In terms of technique, the young players in the County had a great guy to sit down and study. Technically he is perfect.

No one trains harder than him and he is a great accumulator of runs. But he certainly wasn't the ideal captain because he wasn't the right sort of bloke. A pity, for Geoff and for Yorkshire.

I've been told that he made himself into a good cricketer. I talked to people who played against him in their youth. Barry Knight was one of them; he was one of my mentors. He said that Boycott was a stodgy player; he had no shots and didn't look like being the great cricketer he undoubtedly eventually became. Just through sheer hard work and persistence he made himself into a very good player. However, his own character probably has not allowed him to come to terms with the fact that it is a team game. The individual is there to do well as an individual but the ultimate goal is for the team. It has to be; there can be no other way. But Geoff never understood that. He has batted for himself all through the years. The individual should do as well as he can while never forgetting the most important principle: the team comes first.

It is unfortunate because if Boycott had been a golfer or tennis player you would never have noticed this part of his character. But because he is an individual playing a team game, it stands out that he is so selfish in his attitude.

Geoff has become a bit of a folk hero in Yorkshire; there is so much mystique surrounding the bloke. No one really knows him; no one has been allowed to get close to him and he probably hasn't got that many really good mates, especially in cricket circles. That is a shame because Boycott's knowledge is extensive and others could have learned from it.

I suppose many Yorkshire people still love him and feel an affinity towards him because he has been a battler who made good through sheer hard work. The Yorkshire people love that sort of character. But my view is that Boycott must take a major part of the blame for Yorkshire's failure to win anything for almost twenty years, apart from the Gillette Cup in 1969 and the John Player Sunday League in 1983. And they won that Sunday League title while Boycott wasn't playing!

It does seem certain to me that players like Bill Athey might have been established Test match players by now, but for the upheavals in Yorkshire. You don't just up and leave that County, do you? Especially when you are an established first-team player. I would have thought Yorkshire was one of the best Counties to play for and one of the best-paid Counties. Certainly, once you have served your time, your benefit year would produce quite a healthy sum. Therefore, Athey must have gone through a couple of years of inner turmoil about his own cricket and his future and what would be best for him. So he ends up leaving. Yorkshire's loss and Gloucestershire's definite gain in my book because he has had some good results with them.

The contrast between Boycott and Bairstow as captains could not be starker. David Bairstow's captaincy is the classic example of how a guy should lead a side. He is positive, does what is best for the team and has his team-mates' welfare uppermost in his mind. Bairstow is such a character and a real get up and go, rush–rush type of personality that he's the best sort of fellow they could have. You do get a lot of dour Yorkshiremen, but Bairstow has a fair amount of flamboyance. He does seem to worry about the young blokes doing well and he wants them to succeed. You sense that they have every chance of becoming successful again under a guy like that.

Now that Boycott has gone, I have a sneaking suspicion Yorkshire will suddenly become successful once again and start winning trophies. They have so many good young players up there who now have the chance to become established and play regular first-eleven cricket.

Although I didn't see him play, I have heard a great deal about Ashley Metcalfe and people whose views I respect greatly have told me that he could become a terrific batsman. But until now, Metcalfe only got his chances when Boycott was injured, which is no good for a young player trying to make the grade at the highest level. Metcalfe needed a permanent spot there and with it, I think he will get better and better. And so will Yorkshire. The end of all this internal rowing and arguing has to be good for the County. Boycott's departure from the playing side means that at last there will be no atmosphere hanging over the dressing room. The players can get on with the cricket, concentrate totally and, I believe, start being successful. They certainly have a good captain in Bairstow.

In the matches Essex played against them, it was obvious Bairstow had instructed his blokes to go out there and chase the target. I admired him for that. And they went for it right until the death. Under another captain, they might have been prepared to try and shut up shop at 102 for eight against us. But they didn't do that and for me, that positive attitude is what it is all about.

Essex had drawn Nottinghamshire at home in the Benson and

Hedges quarter-finals and had high hopes of making progress into the semi-finals. For all of us it was a major match but especially for myself. A major Cup quarter-final, a place at Lord's in a domestic cricket final just two games away – and the chance to find some form and play a decisive role. The stakes were high, all right!

I had been through bad trots before and you always worry about it. But I am at the stage now, through experience, where I think it *is* just one of those spells you go through and I will come out of it. And I wasn't as worried in the one-day stuff because fortune plays a large part there. But because I was with the new County and an international reputation precedes you, I was expecting big things and I'm sure other people were, too. But it just wasn't working for me this time. I was playing some bad shots; a couple of unlucky things happened, too, and it all added up to comparatively few runs. It was a frustrating time because I really wanted to do well for Essex. Over the last seven years, they have won eight trophies. I didn't want that run to stop all of a sudden because I joined the staff. I don't think I was being too exacting on myself, either. Why shouldn't I demand high standards of myself? I'd built a reputation. Why should I slip below that level of form?

I was reasonably confident that one day I would have a slice of luck and things would start working for me. Your feet start going and you begin to hit the ball a bit better which means you start scoring runs again. If the nets are available I like to get into them to try and work things out and find some better form. But I find in English County cricket you are playing so often that most groundsmen don't prepare net wickets away from the actual playing area. The only place I can think of which is different is Lord's where wickets are sited off the ground. At Chelmsford, we have an artificial wicket with nets around but that is something which detracts from your actual practice. Obviously I prefer turf, but you use whatever facility is available.

Whether I am in Australia, England or any place, I normally take the opportunity to go into the nets, whether I am batting well or not at that particular time. I try and analyse where I am going wrong. Sometimes it is just a good ball which has dismissed you and so you sit down and tell yourself that and say there was not much you could do about it. You may realize there is something wrong – perhaps your feet are not moving properly, or in my case if I am not playing well, I tend to fall across myself a bit to the offside, trying to cover my off stump. But if the ball is coming back at you, you get yourself into some sort of a problem doing that.

With my technique, I try and make sure I am standing up fairly straight because I do have that habit of falling across my stumps. There were little things I knew I was doing wrong but it is very hard when you get out into the middle, to put them right. It takes a long innings to sort it all out and get you flowing again and doing the correct things. But I hadn't had the opportunity to find out about that.

Certainly, I am always trying to analyse my game, trying to make it better. But at the present stage in my career, I have a certain scoring zone and I have tried to keep within those limitations, rather than be too extravagant with shots, which I have been guilty of in the past. But nowadays, I have settled on a certain technique and I have faith in it. I do believe that on certain days I will score runs.

Had I been taking my problems home with me? Partially, I suppose. But I would tend to take home my worries rather more in Test cricket. Anyway, with experience, you tend to grow out of the situation where you come in the dressing room and throw your bat down and sulk for hours and hours on end, if you are playing badly.

I never actually like getting out, no matter how many I have scored. Even if it is 150, I still get a bit cranky with myself for getting out. I am one of those people who are always angry when they get out but I tend to get over it pretty quickly; within, say, half an hour or an hour depending on the situation in the game. If you have got out in an important situation it might take a bit longer but once the game has finished, I do not take it home if I can possibly avoid it.

I needed runs – and I had high hopes I would start to get some against Nottinghamshire. Besides, I had something of an old score to settle against Notts' strike bowler, the New Zealander Richard Hadlee. He had been the difference between New Zealand and Australia in two series, home and away, in the 1985–86 season. Now it was my chance to get some revenge for the chaos he caused in those Test matches.

But if Essex needed a good start to win the match, fate decreed otherwise. In fact, our first error came before we all took the field for the opening overs. We misread the wicket. The wickets at

Chelmsford early in the season had had unusual characteristics. From what Fletcher and Gooch told me, they normally have a certain look to them; they tend to be good to bat on first and then get slower and slower as the game goes on, especially in one-day cricket. Throughout May 1986, however, they had a fair amount of bounce and pace in them. So when we looked at the wicket for this match, we thought it looked as though it was going to be quite a good batting track again. In actual fact, it had a lot of pace and bounce right from the start and the Nottinghamshire fast bowlers and medium pacers, Hadlee, Rice, Cooper and Pick all used it well to their advantage. There was also cloud cover and some variable bounce and we struggled to get any sort of grip on the game.

Brian Hardie went early on, and Goochie didn't last too long, making 25. Clive Rice came on and found the edge of Prichard's bat . . . 59 for three. I knew the pressure was on me to get some runs. But I found just the same problem as before – I couldn't really get going at all. Then, when I had 15 and we were 70, Rice got one through my defences. Typically, considering my luck of the time, it hit me on the elbow of all places when I was half forward and the ball nipped back. It could have fallen anywhere but it fell down on to my stumps. Out for 15 and we were 70 for four.

I was very disappointed. We were struggling and I was trying the give the side the authority and base in the middle order to ensure we reached a good score. But my dismissal put us under even more pressure. If I was annoyed when I got out, I was even less delighted when I read one report the following morning, which ran: 'Border, who is currently playing in McEwan's shadow, was yorked by the Nottinghamshire captain.' I didn't need that sort of statement to remind me of how things were going.

The rest of the lads battled well for us but we struggled to reach 195 for nine off our 55 overs. I had not laid the ghost of Richard Hadlee – he bowled his 11 overs and took two for 30; commendable figures. But the other bowlers played their part, too. Andy Pick was the most economical with two for 27 off 11 overs; Clive Rice, the most successful, taking five for 48 from his 11 overs.

Our total was not large but we reasoned that if we got a good start and put them under pressure, anything could happen. And 'anything' did almost happen. Before the close that night, we sent Chris Broad, Tim Robinson and Derek Randall back to the pavilion with only 39 runs on the board. Three excellent scalps – we seemed back in it.

Our new optimism was reinforced the following morning, although by now the wicket had settled down a little bit. It was generally assumed that if Notts were going to win, then Clive Rice had to play a major part. He did make 50 but was then trapped lbw by Gooch; a real captain's blow. Johnson and Birch didn't last long and Notts found themselves at 125 for six. We felt we were slight favourites at that stage, with a very good chance of a great comeback victory. But we had to get Richard Hadlee out.

Fortunately, or unfortunately depending on your viewpoint, I had seen a lot of Hadlee in recent times. He is normally destroying you with the ball rather than the bat. But he is a more than capable batsman if he stands there and gives it a go. And he demonstrated that perfectly now – he whacked us out of the game.

It was like a nightmare slowly recurring in my mind. He had played so well against Australia, mainly with the ball. Now he was doing it against another side I was in, but this time with the bat. Hadlee's innings was the difference between the sides – it won the match, for Nottinghamshire. He smashed 61 not out, which included three sixes and six fours. There was just nothing we could do about it.

If Hadlee had grafted to score that amount of runs then we might have got down to a situation where they needed to score eight or even nine runs an over. Then we could have put him under pressure and he might have got out. But as it was, he came in and hit the ball sweetly right from the word go and they were always able to cruise through to a win.

If I had to write down the top six cricketers in the world at the moment, Hadlee would be right in there with the best. I know most people would tend to go automatically for West Indians in the fast bowling department and discount others. But as a fast bowler, Hadlee is a superb competitor. And then, after that, he is so dangerous with the bat. He doesn't just go in and swing, either; there is a lot more to him than that. He picks the ball to hit very well and when he can play it as it comes and doesn't have the pressure of scoring at nine or ten runs an over, he is awesome. He can pick the right ball and hit it out of the park. He does that regularly. Though perhaps Hadlee has not scored as many runs as he should have done for a guy with his talent.

With his bowling, Richard has such immaculate line and length to go with that pace. He is obviously one of those players who has sat down and worked out the game and how to succeed as far as a fast bowler is concerned. He minimizes his run-up now that he is later on in his life so that he can bowl longer spells, enabling him to play for another few years. Shrewd fellow. He could play on; it is just a matter of whether his desire is there to do that. He varies his pace, too; he has learned the art of fast bowling brilliantly well. As a batsman, you are looking for the odd bad ball that you can put away. But you have to wait a long time for Hadlee to bowl you one. I have had my fair share of trouble with him. He has got me out at times; at others, I have had my successes against him so I suppose we are reasonably even as far as our contests go. But I have the utmost respect for him.

If Hadlee was playing for Australia, England or the West Indies, he would have a lot more support as a bowler. That is not to detract from the New Zealand team, but he has been their linchpin all his career and he has done a magnificent job. Without Hadlee in Australia during our 1985 Test series against New Zealand, we might have won. That might sound a bit odd because they did beat us 2–1 but they really blitzed us in Brisbane, where Hadlee took nine for 52 and six for 71. He ended up taking 33 wickets in a three-match Test series; an absolutely phenomenal figure. You reckon you have done well as a bowler if you clean up 30 wickets in a five-match Test series. Thirty-three in three Tests is incredible and a comment on Hadlee's quality. Then, when we went to New Zealand, he got another pile of wickets. But the point I am making is that without his brilliance, we might have been able to hold our own. We ended up losing three Tests to one of the six against the New Zealanders and Hadlee alone could account for two Test wins in that lot. One man winning Test matches these days is rare, very rare indeed. It does happen – Botham proved it back in 1981 against us.

So Hadlee had given me a disappointing six match series, home and away, against the New Zealanders. And now he had pitched my County out of the Benson and Hedges Cup.

I wasn't making runs, and runs were my chief claim to fame. Without them, I was giving a lightweight performance and no one knew it better than me. I couldn't work out in my mind whether I needed a rest from the game or more cricket to try and get through this awful spell. It had become the worst of my career – I had never been through a period of play in my life in which I had not scored runs for so long.

I checked up the fixture programme for the next week. I tend not to have it all stored in my mind; I prefer to take each game on its own, and think about the next one when we are ready for it. I don't believe in looking ahead very far because there is no point and besides, it might be detrimental to your concentration with the job in hand. And I needed every ounce of concentration I could muster if I was ever going to emerge from this gloomy spell.

The programme told me I had to go away for a week – I was not cheered much by that news. Jane and the children have become such a part of my life that it is always hard to leave them, for whatever period of time. The prospect of a week away, out of luck, out of form, and wondering when if ever this trough was going to end, depressed me. And so did the weather; it was still cold and often wet.

I suppose you would have to say it was human nature but I couldn't help my mind flitting back to Brisbane and those warm beaches ... just a few times. I tried to shut such thoughts out of my mind but it wasn't easy. After all, I hardly had the joys of personal success with Essex to help me forget. We had lost in the quarter-final of a major one-day competition, and once again I felt I had failed to pull my weight.

I glanced at the calendar – it was Friday, 30 May. I packed my bags for the week's trip, for two County Championship games – Derbyshire and Glamorgan – with only one hopeful thought registering in my mind – May was ending. June had to bring something better ... surely.

One thing above all else was certain – things couldn't get a lot worse for me on the playing side. I couldn't fall even further out of form. That change in fortune all cricketers cling to at such times, was my only consolation as I pulled the car out of our drive and headed away from Chelmsford. Surprise, surprise ... it was just starting to rain!

3

'Allan Border has lost it...!'

Little things can make a big difference to a batsman. We're strange
folk, us batters! I found one example of that during the summer of
1985 and it is a good illustration of the point. I had just changed
bat manufacturers from Symonds, an Indian group, to Duncan
Fearnley's. I started to use them from May 1985 and I have already
scored a hell of a lot of runs with them. As soon as I picked up the
Duncan Fearnley bat and started to use it in the nets, it was almost
as though I felt a surge of power. Symonds are not bad bats, by
any means. But I didn't have the same confidence with them. I
know it is an odd thing to say and people will think all cricketers
are loony, or something! But last year when I went out to bat in
those early matches on the Australian tour, I felt that I could hit
the ball over the top with safety. I just felt so good standing there
with this bat Duncan made me.

Maybe it is on the heavy side compared with times gone by but
not that much so. My bats tend to be about 2 lb, 10 oz or 12 oz. So
right from the word go, I had enormous confidence to hit the ball
strongly. And basically every shot I went for came off and I had a
tremendous summer from a very good start. It was all from the
confidence I had with this bat.

And yet the following season, little had gone right for me. Good
bat or not. Perhaps I was ready to be certified! And in the first half
hour of my innings at Derby, it was the same as ever. Anyone
would have been justified in thinking: Allan Border has lost it. It
was a pretty ordinary morning at Derby that Monday: cold with
drizzle trying to fall. We started late with bad light holding us up –

the weather had meant not a ball had been bowled on the Saturday. Nor was it a promising position when I went in. Gooch and Prichard out; Essex 15 for two.

It was a typical Derby wicket – fairly low and slow. It seamed a little and spun a fraction. The Derbyshire attack was ideal to try and make runs against because Michael Holding wasn't playing and they had two bowlers making their débuts. Other bowlers like Miller, Warner and Newman were out through injury. So the rest were not exactly fearsome bowlers; reasonable but not terrifying. Perhaps a good situation for me to get myself back into form. The eternal optimist again, eh!

Early on in my innings, although I toiled away, I was negative. The same old story, in fact. And then I made a conscious effort to say: Blow this, if I'm going to get out, I'll end everyone's misery and start trying to look for shots. I had been prodding around like an old dog for just eight or ten runs in that first hour! I got angry with myself. I said: For God's sake, start hitting the ball. Then right at that moment, I got a long hop which I hoiked away and then I got another, which I pulled quite well. Almost from that point I started to hit the ball better. The spinners came on to bowl and I attacked them to start off with, so they stuck blokes in the deep. That meant I could afford to knock it around and take singles when I wanted. And it started to come. But it was almost desperation which led to it. In that first hour, I had been so unconvincing. So it was kill or cure. And suddenly I was away.

I played pretty well from there on. But at 110, I hit a long hop straight down deep backward square's throat so I was pretty disappointed I got out. I was determined that having been through such a bad time, I was going to keep batting and batting and when Goochie called a halt, I would still be there.

I got out basically straight after reaching a century which I never like doing. Who's a perfectionist? I can hear you saying. Not satisfied? It's not that. It is the best time to bat when you have a hundred to your name because the pressure has gone. You are relaxed, you have done your job as a batsman. Also, we were still chasing bonus points and I wanted to stay in for that. And the thought was in my mind that I wanted to make some bowlers pay for my lean spell. It didn't matter who the bowlers were.

When I reached the 90s, I wasn't nervous; just very determined. There was no way I was going to do anything rash. To reach 100 is a psychological boost. If I had got out at around 90, I would have felt I had blown it. To get 100 was terribly important to me after I had done all that work. But my basic thought process doesn't change very much on that. Sometimes I am prepared to take more risks say from 70 to 100 than I might normally do, but generally I take great care when I'm anywhere near three figures. Why not? It's not every day you reach that mark, is it?

Of course, in a way it is a silly mark and I have no idea who decreed that figure should be the one for all batsmen to aim at. Someone who didn't know much about cricket, I suggest! Because there are times when you've batted brilliantly under difficult circumstances and got 57 or some such total – and you couldn't have done any better. It might be like scoring 200 on another day.

The time lost on Saturday meant the match had to have a contrived outcome if there was to be any sort of a finish. So on Tuesday, Derbyshire declared at their overnight 44 for no wicket, we forfeited our second innings . . . and they needed 257 to win the game. They never looked like doing it. John Lever got five for 32 and 'Charlie' Childs four for 36. They made 140, we earned 20 points and we moved second in the table, six points behind Lancashire with a game in hand.

When I left Derby that Tuesday evening, I felt I had cracked it; I felt good. But each day is a new set of circumstances; bowler, wicket, conditions. So you always start off any day as a new innings. Some players make 100 one day and go out thinking they are 100 not out the next day. But in my view, that is when you run into trouble.

I'd like to mention one of the Derby players who caught my eye, Kim Barnett their captain. He looks a good, well-organized player. He has a load of responsibilities as captain but as a batsman he looked very competent. He likes to get on with the game and hit the ball hard and he has a good range of shots. Watching him play and noticing the scores he has been making, he looks a player capable of performing at a higher level.

Would he be more effective without the captaincy? I don't necessarily think so. Sometimes being captain tends to make you an even more responsible player. If you have this way about you that you are a fairly aggressive player and then they make you captain, it tends to make you more responsible and therefore more effective. You may play longer innings than might normally have been the case.

If Barnett could put together a string of scores, I figure he would have a good chance of playing for England. When the selectors make a change or at least are thinking of making one with the Test team struggling a bit, that is when players like Barnett or Chris Broad need to be making the runs to come into the reckoning. But it's up to the individuals because you don't get anywhere on potential alone. You only get there on what you can actually do.

One of the drawbacks of the English County cricket circuit is that there is so little time for socializing with your opponents. You leave a match and rush off to another; there isn't any time to have a leisurely evening. When you are staying for a night or two, there tend to be various functions 'on' that you have to attend.

For example, after winning at Derby on Tuesday afternoon, we drove all the way down to Swansea in time only for bed. The night you get in is the worst – you're tired after playing all day and then travelling. So you have a few beers and go to bed or get something sent up on room service.

I really thought the County scene would be more social than it really is. Don't get me wrong – I wasn't looking for a good old booze up every night! But I didn't realize there would be quite so much rushing. Your eating habits certainly take a bit of a nosedive because you tend to have rather a lot of take-away type food.

Sitting in the car for miles and miles was no ordeal for me. I travelled a lot with Paul Prichard because he lived near me. So when we travelled, he usually did the driving while I got into the back seat and conked out. No worries, mate – a few miles of that motorway system and I was in the land of never, never! I find I'm now able to sleep in cars a lot better than I used to. It must be all the practice! In fact, it was probably safer for me to sit in the back and let Paul drive because on the few occasions I had to drive, I found myself starting to nod off after twenty minutes. I ended up having to concentrate terribly hard just to stay awake!

But despite some aspects such as these, playing for Essex was a pleasure. And it wasn't proving as hard as I thought it might be. Not up until then, anyway. We had had a bit of sitting around doing nothing early on because of the way the weather was. And that does get boring. There is nothing worse in cricket than sitting about aimlessly watching the rain tumble down. It's the worst part of the game, no matter where you are. You would rather be out there getting beaten, I suppose – well almost, anyway! You become really lazy and idle; you eat too much because you're picking up sandwiches, cups of tea, etc. It becomes a very boring existence.

We had a day at Northampton when it rained. What on earth do you do with yourself, I thought, on a wet day at Northampton? Some of the guys are well organized and prepared for such days. Keith Fletcher carries his fishing rod around with him and if a day is rained off, he'll go off fishing. Supposed to be good for catching fish, isn't it? I don't know, I'm no fisherman.

Fletch doesn't mind about sitting in the rain, fishing! At Northampton, Richard Williams and Allan Lamb went with him. A few of the guys went jogging; some of the others played cards. The rest of us lay around watching a bit of TV, reading the papers. Some went off to the shops to buy things like tapes for their Walkman machines, or books.

I travelled with Paul Prichard so I shared a room with him. We got on very well. He's a young batsman so we often sat down in the evenings and started talking about batting. If I passed on anything to Paul in terms of knowledge, good and well – except when he starts playing for England against Australia! Maybe in the future I'll regret telling him certain things but I just hope that he becomes a good enough batsman to play for England. Certainly on some of his performances against quality bowlers in the early part of the 1986 season, he ought to be on the right road.

Essex faced a Glamorgan side just two points off the bottom of the Championship table, at Swansea. But whoever it had been against, I was determined to get a big hundred this time. I sensed the light was in my game, once again; there wasn't the same heaviness on my shoulders! I wasn't completely out of the wood but I did feel more comfortable and confident with a bat in my hand. And I reckoned if Glamorgan didn't get rid of me quickly, they would have to wait a long while to see me back in the pavilion.

I finished with 150, and we made 366 after being 39 for two early on. This time, I hadn't thrown my wicket away so easily. At 100, I gritted my teeth and took fresh guard. But there was still one disappointment – Glamorgan did not have Greg Thomas in their side. Greg had been called into the England twelve for the First Test with India at Lord's. And from what I had seen of him when he played against us in the Benson and Hedges one-day match at Chelmsford a few weeks earlier, he certainly deserved his place in that England squad.

I was very impressed with him that day. I had been looking forward to batting against him again in the Championship game.

As far as action and pace is concerned, Greg looks to me like the bowler England have been praying for. I believe he is the one fellow your selectors really ought to give consideration to. He has a magnificent action, pace to worry any of the world's best batsmen and it is only a matter of giving him the experience of playing at Test match level. He is really only comparatively new to the game as far as first-class cricket goes and so he needs all the experience he can gain. I sense, too, he might need slightly more careful handling to give him his chance and build up his confidence.

Thomas had a baptism of fire, having to go to the West Indies and bowl at their batsmen and strokemakers. But I would have given him a chance to show what he could do against the Indians. Frankly, I found it a bit perplexing that Thomas was chosen for the twelve at Lord's for the First Test, left out of that team – and then discarded for the remainder of that series! Did the bloke upset a tray of drinks as twelfth man or something! You honestly wonder what goes on in the minds of some selectors, don't you? It wasn't as if England were thrashing the Indians and not needing some strong bowlers. Thomas's pace could have upset a few of the Indian batsmen.

I watched Greg Thomas very closely at Chelmsford and he surprised me. He bowled very, very quickly against us and had Graham Gooch ducking and diving. Now to me, that showed he had a good deal of pace. Medium pacers don't force Goochie to hurry his stroke.

I know Thomas was said to have bowled badly in Trinidad, taking none for 101 off 15 overs. But from what I can gather it was just a lack of experience; the batsmen were taking him on and he didn't know what to do. That will come with more bowling. But with that sort of potential, I think England ought to try and stick with him. England have been crying out for a bloke like Thomas for years but when you get him, you don't seem to have faith in him. You should stand by someone with his potential. Paired together, Greg Thomas and Graham Dilley have the genuine pace to get the best batsmen in the world hopping around a bit. And with experience of playing in Test matches especially together as an opening attack pair, you could have a really strong pace attack in the years to come.

Glamorgan had a bad day against us on the Thursday. We bowled them out for 160 in the first innings and put them in again on the follow-on. By stumps, they were 125 for eight and our only worry was not having finished them off that night when we were so close. You are concerned about rain coming and robbing you of a nice points haul.

That evening, I had a function on at a pub over the road from the Swansea ground. The beer was half price that night and the place was jam-packed. Castlemaine, my employers, like me to go to some of the local pubs to do promotions and I enjoy them. You get a chance to meet some folk from that area and have a yarn over a few pints of the Aussie brew. It's a mighty pleasant way to while away a few hours, especially when you are away on the road for a week. Sitting in hotel rooms has obvious drawbacks so it is always good to get out and meet people.

The next morning, we took only fifteen or twenty minutes to wrap up the rest of the Glamorgan innings. So we won by an innings and 73 runs, taking a maximum 24 points and, in the process, moved to the top of the Championship table, 18 points clear of Lancashire who didn't have a game. It was a highly satisfying end to a successful week, both for the team and for myself. We had won both away matches, taken 44 points and I had scored two centuries. The contrast with seven days earlier, in terms of my mood and expectation, was dramatic.

After a week away, I was delighted to get back home to Jane and the children. Our little girl Nicole is at the age where she changes almost every day. So being away for a whole week, I notice the difference, and it is quite incredible in that time.

You don't notice much change with Dene but at that early age, they have special little ways of looking at you or different mannerisms. It was a tug to go away from them. I was coming to terms with it a little bit better than I did initially. I was doing something I have got to do. After all, I will not be playing cricket all my life, so I can spend heaps of time with them in a few years. So I am hoping the little bits and pieces I am missing out on now, I can catch up with later.

I have spent so much time away from home in recent years that it is a delight to get home for a while. Jane copes with everything incredibly well, better than a lot of women would. She has, of course, two children to keep her fully occupied now but I never get too many hassles or too many teary phone calls or that kind of thing, about being away. So we have a pretty good system going. It works out well and I'm quite lucky in that respect.

Jane is a good traveller and she enjoyed going to all the country houses and cathedrals there are in England. She is the ideal tourist, whereas I'm not. I will look at one or two cathedrals but that will be it. Jane is more one for going into all the history of things. She will read books on the Plantagenets and the Kings and Queens of England. She really is into English history and heritage. That is great for her because Australian history is obviously limited. Going to England was quite fascinating.

Away for a week, now Essex had two weeks at home. The relief of picking up a bat and expecting to make some runs was almost as good a feeling as being home with the family. Even the weather seemed about to improve. We started our match against Nottinghamshire at Chelmsford on 7 June in bright sunshine, even if the wind was still pretty cool. But our start was enough to warm up every Essex supporter.

Notts won the toss but lost five men for just 67. When Hadlee was also out making them 129 for six, we felt we might have them out for around 170, perhaps 180. But then Johnson came in and turned the whole innings upside down. He made 128, didn't give a single chance and Notts reached 299. That was a big score on that wicket because it looked like giving the bowlers some assistance. Gooch and Pringle were away at the Test and we lost Gladwin and Hardie in making 42 by the close. I was there, 13 not out with Paul Prichard who was on 16. I felt set up for the challenge ahead. I was keen to make some runs, as the experienced middle-order batsman. They were needed and I had been in good form all week. I proved it again on the Sunday in the John Player match against Notts. We made 190 and I top scored with 58.

But after beating Notts by 11 runs in the Sunday game, to go to the top of that table, too, things went wrong the next morning. It is always in my mind on a Monday morning that it is seldom easy picking up the threads of a three-day County Championship game. The big crowd from the Sunday has shrunk to a small Monday morning gathering; the game is different, the approach is altogether new. And yet you have to force your mind back to what happened on the Saturday, not the events of the previous day. Getting your mind sorted out in the right direction is not straight-forward. It is inevitable you are still thinking of the Sunday match events but it is no good whatsoever going out to bat thinking of another game, another day.

45

I went out that morning but was soon back. I didn't even add to my overnight score – and I wasn't that pleased. Eddie Hemmings bowled me one which nipped through and hit me on the pad. I didn't think the ball was straight enough to have hit the wicket but the umpire put his finger up. Considering the situation we were in, I was disappointed at the decision and at getting out. I felt I'd let the lads down.

So 44 for three became even worse; 50 for four, 70 for five and 94 for seven. We didn't even look like saving the follow-on. But Paul Prichard had stayed through all this and made batting look easy at his end. An attack containing Richard Hadlee, Clive Rice, Kevin Cooper, and Eddie Hemmings is not the worst around. But Prichard batted beautifully, making 147 not out and taking us right up to 240. Hemmings bowled with great control and poise, taking seven for 102 off 42 overs. But by the close Nottinghamshire had stretched their lead to 216, with Derek Randall making a fine 60. They set us 293 to win but we ran out of time at 222 for five. At least I made 50 this time although Paul Prichard again took the honours with a superb 78.

The draw was enough to keep us on top of the table and some of the lads who had come into the side had shown their value with good performances. Charlie Childs had bowled ever so well in the past week or two and he did his bit with the bat, too, at the end of our first innings against Notts, by making 11 and helping Prichard add 26 for the last wicket. At that stage of the game, those were crucial runs.

The semi-finals of the Benson and Hedges Cup that week meant we had three days off. I was glad for a rest and an ease up after almost a fortnight of constant, day-in, day-out cricket. So I sat at home and heard how Middlesex wiped away Nottinghamshire's challenge for a place in the final, wondering how we might have done if it had been us going to Lord's for the semi-final. If only ... !

4

Gunning for Gower

At about the time Essex's Championship match with Nottinghamshire was petering out into a draw, events at Lord's were taking a thoroughly strange and puzzling turn. England had lost to India in the first of the Cornhill Test series, their sixth successive defeat following the 5–0 whitewash by the West Indians in the Caribbean the previous winter.

David Gower was summarily dismissed as England captain, just after a TV interview which inevitably brought up the question of his own future. David must have known what was about to happen and he must have felt sickened by it. But he retained his dignity to the last; something which didn't surprise me a jot. I had come to know and respect David Gower greatly, especially from our positions as rival captains in the Ashes series in England during 1985.

David and I had been friends for a long while because our careers had tended to run fairly parallel. There were other little similarities, too; like the similar amount of runs we had scored and the way we had experienced lean spells. We took over the captaincy of our countries at about the same time and went through the same sort of dramas. So bearing all that in mind, you could imagine my amazement when I reached England back in April and started reading in the papers, almost from day one, that David Gower should no longer be England cricket captain. Why the hell not? was my first reaction. Who would have made such a difference that England would have won the series in the West Indies?

The papers persisted and were full of it. They said David Gower was not the right bloke for the job; he was too laid back, too easy going. England lost in the West Indies and everyone said it was a disgrace. They said it was time someone different was appointed.

I regarded all that as sheer narrow-mindedness, nothing else. Because when I had left England the previous September as Australian captain, we had lost the Ashes series 3–1 and although we got a reasonable amount of flak once we got home, it was a fairly understanding type of press we received. Over in England at that time, David Gower was the greatest thing since sliced bread. He had won the Ashes back for England, he had led you to victory in India after going one-down which is never an easy thing to do there ... and he had scored 700-odd runs in the Test series against us. After failing twice in the first Test at Headingley (something anyone can do there), he made some absolutely phenomenal scores – 86 and 22, 166 and 17, 47, 215 and finally 157 at The Oval. I thought I'd had a reasonable series with the bat, scoring 597 runs from eleven innings at an average of 66. But from only nine innings, David made 732 runs for an average of 81. It was remarkable scoring by the standards of any Test cricketer, past or present.

With that batting form behind him and the Ashes regained, everything was looking rosy for the West Indies tour. I made the comment at the time that if the batting could hold up to the challenge ahead from the West Indies' quick bowlers, England would have a very good chance. You have to overcome the pace barrage otherwise they just steamroller you.

It is history now but the batting just wasn't up to it. The pace was relentless and West Indies dominated because of that. But from what I read and from what I could see on TV, Gower's captaincy didn't make any difference to the final outcome of any of the games. Not at all. It would not have mattered who was captain, they would have suffered the same fate. The West Indians were far too good and the wickets were unpredictable in pace and bounce. When you are playing against that sort of calibre of bowling you have got basically no chance because their batting is not placed under any pressure. So Gower goes out into the field with his side having made 150 of which he has probably got 50, and what sort of a plan have you got?

Gower finished top of the batting averages; he did his level best. But when the West Indians bat, they come out swinging and chasing quick runs because they know you have made only 150 or 180. So if they make 250 to 300, they will steamroller you again for around 150. There is never any pressure on them. That was the chief problem David faced as captain of that team. At no stage was he able to lead from the front and that is something I have found during my career as captain. You are always leading a team from behind; you are always in positions where you are trying to get out of trouble in a Test match, rather than trying to generate positive things. It is so different when you are in front; you are trying to get blokes out, you can afford attacking fields with lots of close to the wicket catchers.

That was the difference in Gower's captaincy during the Ashes series. Once England got the sniff of victory and started to gain the upper hand, David's captaincy got better and better because he was able to dictate terms.

Now how the people of England, or especially the selectors, can have expected him to have done any differently, is all beyond me. How they expected Mike Gatting to do much better, is also a mystery to me.

I believe Gower's sacking was one of *the* most tragic decisions I have ever seen in my life; the guy was made a scapegoat for his team-mates' poor performances. His own performances in the West Indies were O K; he justified his selection in the team, yet it seems his captaincy suffered only because of this inability to lead from the front. But I defy any selector to say who would have changed that situation. And besides, against this present West Indian side, that is no disgrace at all.

The wickets in the Caribbean were so uneven, that was the chief problem. About as flat and smooth as the Andes, some joker said! O K, New Zealand drew two Tests out there the previous year in 1985. But then the wickets were reliable, that's what you must remember.

When I played there, Australia lost 3–0 in a five-Test series and it should have been 4–0. But the wickets were good, very good on that tour. So, you see, we weren't exactly pulling up many trees in terms of great results even though we had good pitches.

In fact, the wickets had been so good on our tour, that when I came back and saw Gooch and Gower during 1985 for that Ashes series, I told them the best place to play the West Indies was in the Caribbean because the wickets were so reliable. That was a joke in the light of what followed! They must have wanted to throttle me!

That, obviously, wasn't the case with this last tour; one ball would go low, the other would climb into the air. No side anywhere in the world can do anything if that is happening. Even the West Indies. To blame England's captain for losing a series under those conditions is ridiculous.

Another factor was that England didn't play in Guyana. New Zealand did, and made 440 there. The wicket is a beauty and I don't think there has been a result on it in years. But on the wickets which had pace and bounce, New Zealand got rolled over just like everyone else.

But as for the England captaincy, I find it a strange situation. We have a different set up in Australia; there is no way in the world I am appointed captain for the whole Australian summer. The people in charge don't have that sort of faith in me! I get the captaincy for the particular match which is next. And when the Test comes round after that, hopefully I am captain again. But there's no guarantee about it. If they wanted to make a change, they would do so for the next Test and I would be out of the team. Hard lines stuff! We pick our team first and then the captain after that and I've got to say I believe that's a far better way of doing it.

The idea in England seems to be that the captain is given a Test series in which to succeed. But with David Gower, the selectors didn't even follow their own rules. Perhaps they were that baffled by that stage! What should have happened was that Gower should have been given the entire series against India to prove that he could still dictate terms as the captain. Or, if they wanted to, sack him straightaway.

The compromise the selectors came up with was wrong, in my book. A guy who had done what David Gower had for his country, deserved better treatment. To get the two one-day internationals and just one Test, was downright unfair. You know the old neck is on the block with the guillotine poised just above so that it will fall if anything goes astray.

As it was, the Indians just played an extremely good, competent series and beat England. But was Gower's captaincy at fault? I doubt it. It might seem strange to some of my Aussie mates for me to be defending a Pommie. But I believe Gower was badly treated. I felt real sympathy for the guy. He came out of it with his head held high. But I'm not sure you could say that about everyone who played a part in the episode.

I know the job of captain isn't an easy one anywhere. But in

England the people seem to take great pleasure in knocking winners down once they are on top. I was really interested to see the outcome of it all because I didn't for one moment really believe the selectors would sack Gower. I thought they would give him the rest of the series, at worst. I felt the attitude ought to have been: Let's hang on; we've had a few dramas, let's get things back on an even keel and see what Gower can do in the entire series against the Indians. But no, they go and sack Gower, and then his deputy, Gatting, loses the next match and with it the series. Yet he keeps the job. About as consistent as the English weather!

I know the criticism of Gower is that he is too laid back. And sure, he does have that approach to everyday life. He tends to see the humorous side of things fairly easily rather than get too morbid about situations. That's the way he plays his cricket. He is always looking to force the scoring rate regardless of the situation. And anyway, with regard to his laid back approach, the selectors ought to have known all about that before they appointed him in the first place. It wasn't as if the guy became a different character after he'd been in the job. He was always like that. It wasn't David Gower who changed but the selectors' attitude to him. And that's a shame.

To me, Gower is a bloody good competitor. He is not just going to give you his wicket by any means. He is a tougher character inside than he shows outside. Going back to the West Indies tour, the other guys were Test cricketers and if they didn't want to put the effort in at practice and contribute to the side as such, without having some figure such as the captain whipping them into shape, then they were not really worthy of their position. That's my view of it, anyway. The players who failed were the ones who should have been on the line facing the bullet for the shambles. And yet Gower was made the scapegoat for their failure. Gower didn't lose 5–0, England did. Some justice, eh!

Good practice is vital. The trouble is that you can reach a certain point where if you practise and practise badly, you are sometimes better off not doing so at all. And if the facilities are not there to have a good practice then maybe you are better off just lying on the beach having a good rest and trying to come to terms with what you are faced with. Sometimes total relaxation and getting away from it all is far better therapy.

But poor form wasn't the only trouble with England's 1985–86 tour; there were too many undercurrents involved. Graham Gooch was having alarms and the South African blokes, that is the other players who had been there, were inevitably involved. Matches were boycotted by some spectators; the whole thing wasn't right from the start. The Antiguan official, Lester Bird, kept sounding off about having these players in the country or not having them. So obviously Goochie did not enjoy himself out there and that would have had a bad effect on his team-mates. The whole tour seemed to me to start off on a very sour note with all the political stuff.

If I had been there with that politician ranting on and making capital out of the situation, I would have seriously considered packing up and coming home. And I mean that. Gooch went to South Africa, rightly or wrongly. He served his time out of the Test side and now he is back in it.

The West Indies officials or any politicians cannot dictate to any country who is chosen and who is left out. They are playing a dangerous game. I certainly don't think we should allow those countries to dictate to us. To me, if they had said at the start: 'If Gooch comes over here all this will happen,' then if I had been in charge of England, I would have sent a note back saying: 'Fair enough, we will not tour.'

Most of the problems are caused by politicians or administrators. The cricketers themselves just want to get on and play the game. West Indians, and their politicians especially, need cricket because it is the religion of the region. If it got out that the England team wasn't coming because the Prime Minister or some official of a country said he didn't want such and such a player due to South African connections, I don't think the people would accept that.

After all that lot, Botham was getting hounded by the British press. Around that second and third Test time, when the series was already lost, morale must have been terribly low.

Curiously, Australia don't seem to have the same sort of trouble in the West Indies. We toured with Kepler Wessels and it was all sorted out before we went. Wessels even went into Guyana and we played a Test match there. Yet you couldn't do that because Gooch was in the side. Frankly, the whole thing is crazy and I don't understand it. Wessels is South African, born and bred. Yet they allow him in. If it came to the crunch and the West Indian politicians said they didn't like me, then I'd flatly refuse to go.

As for practice facilities, we seemed able to organize ourselves. We went to other grounds although they certainly were not always good. But we also had a lot of relaxation time and we were losing Test matches. When we had to practise, we did so and hard, making do with what there was available. You just hope your inter-island games give you a good practice for the Tests.

The last time I was there, I had a good tour personally. And we also had an enjoyable time – except for the results! We lost the Test series 3–0 but still managed to come away reasonably happy with the tour itself, not so much with the results. We certainly didn't have any of the disturbing incidents which followed the England tour there. I should think the English blokes almost fought each other to get on board the plane for the flight home! That's a shame because tours ought to be enjoyable.

It is my firm belief that too many countries have been too lax with the West Indies in recent years. I just don't see why they should dictate terms. They are a very good cricket side at the moment and they are beating everyone. But in my book that doesn't give them a right to dictate how the game should be played in England, Australia or anywhere else. The fact is this – they need England and Australia to survive themselves.

Tours by those countries to the West Indies are great money-spinners and keep the game financially alive in the Caribbean. So we are in a stronger position to dictate terms when it comes down to simple economics. Therefore, we should be much stronger in pursuing what we believe in.

For example, I think the question of having a statutory number of overs a day in a Test match, should be an ICC decision. The West Indies have their committee member but if the ICC votes by whatever it is to one, then you have a case to force the West Indies to accept a certain number of overs when they go abroad for a Test series. I think that if you go to a country you should comply to the requirements of that country. If we go to the West Indies, we accept their pitches, rules and regulations. Maybe if they don't want a minimum requirement over there, OK, you don't play it. But when they come to us if we insist on a certain number of overs, that should be it.

I am certainly in favour of a minimum number of overs per day. Because with a team like the West Indies, if you did ever look like beating them which admittedly is not so likely at the moment, they could slow the game down to a ridiculous pace like nine or ten overs an hour. Don't tell me it would never happen – it has, in India. They had a stage where they bowled about eight or nine overs in one hour, once. I have played cricket in India and it is ridiculous there – sometimes you are getting only 70 or 75 overs in a day's play. That's crazy – the people are just not getting value for their money under those circumstances. The game should be about getting a result because in this day and age that is what people want. At least if spectators know they are going to get 90 overs in a day, they have something guaranteed. And I feel that figure is about the right compromise between limited-overs cricket and the five-day Test stuff.

The rate of 118 which was used in English County cricket a few seasons back, was far too many. But 110 is good; it encourages teams to hustle in the field and to use spinners. It is a good mark for County cricket. In Australia it is different because it is a harsher climate in which to play the game. So you get a drinks break every hour and that takes up further time. But 110 overs is too many in a Test match because there is a lot more pressure and consequently you need much more time to think over things. Field placings, bowling; the whole pace of the game does slow down because you have more time in which to get a result.

In my experience 90 overs is about the mark for a day's play in Tests. If you particularly want to bowl more than that, it's up to you as the fielding side. There is always that avenue there for you. But on the other hand, and this is probably the most critical aspect, you cannot slow the game down anymore than having to bowl 90 overs. A minimum requirement is good.

Because the West Indies are such a good side and have four fast bowlers steaming in at you, all these different issues come up. It is like the use of the bouncers. There was never any restriction in times gone by about limited use of the bouncer or minimum number of overs. And to be perfectly honest, I believe that if England or Australia had a similar pace battery, we would be arguing along the West Indies' lines that if we want to bowl only 70 overs in a day or send down three bouncers in one over, well tough luck.

Perhaps it's a little selfish on our part to give the West Indies a hard time because they have such a remarkable cricket team. It is up to those countries to come to terms with it in the best way they can. For instance, wicket preparation and their own talent. Just because they are better than you doesn't mean you should try to change the rules too much. But in the case of overs I do feel there is a genuine reason for insisting on 90 a day.

People have often asked me whether I think the West Indies will always have so many good fast bowlers. God, I hope not, is my first reaction! After all, you can reel off the obvious names like Holding, Marshall, Garner and Patterson and still list plenty of others like Clarke, Gray, Walsh, Croft, etc. I do believe they will always have the pace. But whether they will become as good bowlers, is something we shall probably find out very soon. Andy Roberts and Michael Holding started off this current era, then Joel Garner slotted in. They have always had a host of others from which to choose the fourth man. Now, Malcolm Marshall is the spearhead. They have had a lot of other talent and being in the same side bowling with those others must have helped the fourth pace man, no end.

But look ahead a little and imagine a situation where there was no Marshall, Holding or Garner. Then, the blokes who had filled in as the fourth string, would be the No. 1 and 2. Could they cause the same sort of havoc? I wonder . . .

Personally, I don't think they will. I believe the West Indies might struggle more when those exceptional bowlers have gone. Why? You must remember that bowlers like Holding, Garner and Marshall are not run of the mill quick bowlers – they are brilliant quickies who can do things with the ball. They don't just tear in and slam the thing down – they possess an art which is about swinging and moving the ball.

We might not see their like again for some years to come.

5

A plundering of riches in reverse

There is no doubting the impact and entertainment factor provided in English County cricket by overseas stars. For instance, how about this little teaser for a quiz question of the future ... What do the West Indian cricketers Malcolm Marshall, Clive Lloyd, Patrick Patterson, Gordon Greenidge, Michael Holding and Viv Richards all have in common? Well, you take it as read that they're all superb competitors, the lot of them. And it also goes without saying that they have blitzed just about every side they have come up against in Test cricket in recent years, with either bat or ball. Or, in many cases, with both. But the answer is, they have all grown up and nurtured their games for the top level, in the environment of English County cricket. Great for them, great for West Indies cricket. But I'm not so sure it's as good for the rest of the cricketing world.

It seems that English County cricket has helped make West Indian cricket the strongest it has probably ever been. And the system here is keeping West Indies cricket on top of the world. So a handful of stars, however great, aren't enough to prove the point, you say? Well, to the first list, how about adding another, about as long and virtually as good. Gordon Greenidge, Courtney Walsh, Roger Harper, Colin Croft, Sylvester Clarke, Lawrence Rowe, Winston Davis. Yet another formidable cluster of names. In my time as a Test match cricketer, just about every one has given the side I've been playing in some headaches at various times.

Of course, other players have come from all over the world to play English County cricket. Pakistanis, Indians, Aussies (although relatively few, by comparison) and lots of South Africans. But it just so happens, very unfortunately for world cricket, that the young West Indians are very fast learners. They're not only excellent athletes who can bowl quickly but in England they learn how to play the game professionally. Fair dinkum, they listen, watch, learn. Quickly. And then unleash all that acquired knowledge on opponents in the Test match arena. It sure makes life difficult for other nations around the world who come up against the guys from the Caribbean.

The mentor of all those guys is probably Clive Lloyd, to my mind, the man who has done most to put West Indies cricket where it is. On top of the pile. I've had some great battles with sides Lloydie has been in, and I've built up a deep respect for the man. Not only for what he has done for his country but also up at Lancashire. I don't find it hard to understand why they treat him like a God in those parts. Look at the man's achievements and loyalty over eighteen years with the county.

But 'Big Cat' is also a tough, shrewd cookie; he's nobody's fool. And I wouldn't put it past Clive to be thinking about the next ten years of West Indies cricket, even now he has retired. He is a forward thinker, like I say, an astute man. So he has even been quoted as saying to his young players at home: 'Go to England and learn the game.'

It makes sense, too. There is no better grounding for a young player than to go over to England. I realize that now – I've seen it at first hand. When I get back to Australia, I'll be talking to guys like Greg Ritchie and young Steve Waugh, telling them to think about going to England. It would help them a hell of a lot. In this environment, you've got to become a better, more mature player.

You learn how to play the game under different conditions and in various circumstances. After a few years in County cricket, your education is all but complete. You have faced fast bowling from the world's best; slow bowling, typical pressures. And you've done it on as many different kinds of wickets as you could imagine.

For the young fast bowlers of the West Indies, it's a sort of plundering of riches, in reverse. The English used to sail to the Caribbean to do their plundering. Now the Caribbean quickies come into England's backyard to do the same, but in a cricketing sense. A couple of seasons here soon sorts out for those young bowlers where they should bowl on a good wicket, a bouncy wicket, a slow wicket; a wicket which is helpful or one that's a hindrance. They learn to bowl a line and length.

Then when they come up for Test selection, they come into the side like Patrick Patterson did recently and just blitz you. There is no learning process in the Test match arena for them – they've done their learning against world-class batsmen, in English County cricket. By then, they're ready to give problems to the best batsmen in the world.

What is the answer? Well, although I don't think it's a silly suggestion that overseas players might be eliminated altogether in the future, I don't consider it a practical solution. You've got to remember the spectator and sponsor; both play a vital role in the modern-day game. Would a County's sponsors be quite so happy to put their hands in their pockets, if their overseas stars were no longer with them? I doubt it.

So to be sensible, there has to be a compromise. Maybe a greater turnover of overseas players would be better. Perhaps you could restrict them to so many years on the staff. I'm not sure. But I do back the TCCB in this. They have started a trend towards only one overseas player per County and I'm convinced that's a move in the right direction. Why? Well, it will force Counties to bring on their own young talent. And that has to be good in the long term for English Test cricket.

You can't really expect the English cricket fan to accept the sudden loss of every brilliant overseas star. Anyway, it would put awful pressures on County finances. But at the moment, the balance is too much the other way; overseas players dominate too much in England.

Look at a County like Nottinghamshire. Clive Rice and Richard Hadlee are two of the best all-rounders in the world. One bats at No. 4, the other at No. 6 or 7. And they both open the bowling, although Ricey not so much recently through injury. But they are, in effect, taking up four places. And if you're a kid who fancies himself as a good bat or a useful quick bowler in Notts' Second Eleven, you must wonder when you're going to displace guys like those two. See the problem?

Really, you only have to go back to the 1950s and 1960s when there were not many overseas players playing County cricket and you see that English Test cricket was strong. You can draw your own conclusions from that.

As an Australian, it would concern me if our State sides contained so many players who had no chance of playing for Australia. But that is the situation in England. Some English counties have as many as five or six players who won't play cricket for England in the future, either because they are overseas players or they're too old. It looks like most counties have two or three players who have a real chance of making it into the Test side here. The rest wouldn't or couldn't. Therefore, I reckon the percentage is wrong.

Looking after sponsors and spectators is fine but not to the detriment of your own standards at international level. And I'd say that has been happening in recent years.

I know that in Australia the chief aim of our State cricket is to foster young talent for our Test side. OK, you might say, what's gone wrong in recent years? Well, something similar to what happened to you when England lost players to South Africa. You had a lean time. And we've found a similar problem. But your domestic game surely should be about training young players for the English Test team. Not the West Indies Test side!

Talking about Australia, it's interesting to compare the youngsters I came up against in England and their attitudes to the game, to those in Australia. Personally, I'm a player with an inbuilt competitive spirit. I hate getting out, at any time. Folk who turn up expect you to do well. And why not? They've paid their money, they are entitled to expect some entertainment. I think I've always hated getting out in cricket. Even back in those vital 'Test' matches we played as kids in our backyard, at home in Sydney. But I dislike being dismissed even more nowadays. It doesn't matter who has got me out.

The guy can be the best in the world, or a part-time donkey-drop bowler who induces a mistake by me. I still get upset about being out. Even after I've made centuries, I'm always a little cranky with myself for playing a bad shot. But I don't always see the same intensity in others. And I don't know whether that's right or wrong. Whether it's that I'm being over intense or too worried about failure, I'm not sure. But you can only be the way you are. And I'm not about to apologize for the way I feel when I'm dismissed. Frankly, it hurts. And the lesser the form of cricket, the more nervous I get about performing well. When I go back to play club cricket in Australia, I'll walk out to bat knowing everybody expects me to score 100. That's real pressure, perhaps more, surprisingly enough, than when you face the West Indies in a Test.

People don't expect a ton from you every time you face those guys.
I can't think of a batsman in the world who would be expected to
score like that.

But in minor cricket at home, they do. After all, you're the
guy with the big name reputation. Why shouldn't they anticipate
something special? So when I look at others, I'd like to think
they, too, burn with desire to do well for themselves. But more
importantly, for the team they are representing. But I do look at
young players sometimes and think they haven't got the same
desire. Maybe that's unfair, I don't know. Perhaps youngsters have
more in their lives these days than just cricket. If so, that's a
shame. When I was young, you lived for the game. I and my two
brothers played for hours and hours. We'd represent Australia,
against England. And we'd dream of the day we'd walk out at
Lord's or the Sydney Cricket Ground to bat for Australia in an
Ashes Test. Nothing wrong with that, in my book.

There is no doubt that a lot of young cricketers have been getting
opportunities in recent Australian Test teams, that normally
wouldn't have come close to it. Not because they're no good. Just
because of events taking place.

Australia has gone through a situation where our Test side has
been decimated. First, by retirements; then by the South African
affair. And you don't replace players like Ian and Greg Chappell,
Dennis Lillee and Rod Marsh instantly. Guys of that quality don't
come up in the night, like mushrooms, ready to be picked the next
morning. And we also lost a stack of others: Bruce Laird, Bruce
Yardley, Geoff Dymock. Then there were the South African depar-
tures; players like Terry Alderman, Carl Rackemann and Steve
Smith.

Suddenly, our cricket was in turmoil. Picking Test teams became
a nightmare. Of course, we'll get through it. That is guaranteed.
But I just hope that the kids who have been thrust into the breach
see it as a fantastic opportunity to cement themselves into a pretty
good lifestyle. But I do wonder whether they have the desire or
desperation to do well and grab the opportunity with both hands.
I guess only time will tell.

In England youngsters have a superb learning process before
they reach the Test match stage. I look at a young man like Paul
Prichard, my batting mate at Essex. He's playing in the same side
as four guys who played Test cricket for England in 1986 – Gooch,
Foster, Pringle and Lever.

I was also in there, having replaced a superb South African batsman, Kenny McEwan. And Paul has already had a couple of years alongside players like that. He started off under a great skipper, Keith Fletcher. It must be superb to come up with players of that quality and experience if you're twenty or twenty-one. It is a fantastic gounding for a youngster playing the game over here and aiming to reach Test match level. He won't fail for lack of advice or know-how close at hand.

Whereas in Australia, our twenty-year-olds, if they reached the standard Prichard is at now, would probably be playing Test cricket. That's the difference. Paul's education will be a lot tougher. If he does reach the Test team, he'll know all about the ups and downs. He'll understand exactly what it takes to become a good player. He's lucky he hasn't been thrust forward far too early like some of our boys. But circumstances have thrown it up, as I've said.

OK, in some cases, that's an advantage. You find out very early who can play and who can't. But it's not so straightforward for the kids. And Test cricket takes a bit of getting used to, even if you're a highly experienced performer. So if you're a kid, it's nice to be nursed along for a few years before facing the ultimate challenge of Test match cricket.

But while appreciating that, it is sometimes the way we accept defeat which makes me wonder whether these lads really have the same desire to succeed, the way we fold under pressure, or had done anyway in the previous twelve months. When we are playing well, these youngsters look world beaters. But I always reckon you learn about people when things are not going well for you.

You're chasing a bit of leather in the field, or under pressure with the bat. Or you've lost a match. That's when you look at blokes' faces and see whether they are really hurting inside. For me, the feeling eats away inside when we lose. I hope my mates are feeling the same way.

I remember from my school days, the old saying about 'Captains courageous'. But from my limited experience of the job, I'd say 90% of it is down to luck. If that sounds like a heretic talking in the estimation of intellectuals like Mike Brearley, then I'm sorry. But you speak from personal experience, don't you?

Captaincy is also partly to do with psycho-analysis. Judgement, I'd put at no higher than 10%! I do honestly believe luck plays as big a part as that. As captain, you've got to make sure everyone is locked into the primary ambition of winning. But if all your lads are in a positive frame of mind and the old homework has been done on the opposition players, then you can captain almost by textbook.

It's fairly straightforward. OK, you can make some inspired moves at times, but I'd say my job is mainly about getting the best out of my players. That can be tiring, geeing everyone up.

Perhaps that's why I enjoyed not being skipper during my season with Essex. It was good to have that responsibility taken from me. It's not that I had been disinterested – very far from it. Try keeping A.B. out of a game of cricket! I found myself like a frustrated car driver at times, pushing his foot down on imaginary pedals in the passenger seat! And I yelled out at Goochie or Fletch to try this or that, at various stages. But I think they welcomed it. Well anyway, they weren't too rude in telling me to shut up! Occasionally they'd say: 'A. B., have you any thoughts?' If I was on the field and I started motioning that some guy was too fine or whatever, they could either take heed or ignore it – that was fine by me. But I can't help it. I want to be in the game.

I think everyone should do that because the skipper isn't the only guy out there representing the side. Others should chip in. I'm a real democrat when it comes to captaincy – free speech, say what you like, sort of stuff. OK, I'm the guy who has to make the final decision when I'm captain. But you should be able to ask your mate what he thinks and expect some sane suggestion, rather than a smart aside to the effect that it's your problem, you solve it, mate! Hell, it's a difficult enough job. All advice welcome.

6

A dulled appetite for the game

I sure could have used some advice before I arrived in England in April, about the little ways and means of County cricket. At times, they amazed me! Some of the things you guys get up to would be enough to render Dame Edna speechless.

For instance, I've never ever played in games before where a side forfeits its innings. And nothing could have prepared me for the sight of batsmen, who had hardly bowled seriously in their lives, coming on in County games and lobbing up donkey drops, as though they were on the beach teaching their youngsters how to bat. Gee, I had to look twice the first time it happened. I simply couldn't believe my eyes!

Early on, I had to ask a mate what the hell was going on. These blokes called batsmen were bowling rubbish stuff at Test match cricketers. And my side was being smacked all over the field. You'd have a bloke giving away 50 or 60 runs from four or five overs. And I'd be thinking: Hey, hold on there; those are first-class runs you're messing about with! Of course, it's all about striving for results. Because of the weather and the fact that three-day games are played in England, whereas it's four-day cricket in Australia, you run out of time, on various occasions. And you indulge in, I think the term is, manufactured cricket.

Overseas, you do sometimes set up a run chase. But it's virtually unheard of for a side to give a bloke 40 or 50 runs in five overs or so, just to make sure they have enough runs to set you a target. I thought 'gimmies' were something you came across on the golf course, not the cricket field!

I find that situation false, because when you look at the averages at the end of the year, they don't tell a true story. If a bloke just happens to be lucky enough to be batting when all this is going on, he could get the fastest century of all time. In my book, that wouldn't be justified. Yet it's still called first-class cricket and they're first-class runs. But isn't it messing around with the rules and ideals of the game a bit too much? I suppose the answer is that it's better to have a game being played out for a result than trying just for bonus points.

In Australia, we wouldn't do it because we look at our first-class cricket as a breeding ground for our Test match players. So it is not of paramount importance to play the game solely for the spectators. It is more to make sure the players are getting a good grounding in first-class cricket. Then they can play Test cricket properly.

The only value I can see to a bloke in getting loads of donkey drops lobbed up at him, is if he's likely to face the same sort of stuff from Michael Holding or Joel Garner in a Test match he might play in! And as we all know, the chances of that are about as slim as us Aussies losing the taste for cold beer! Remote, in a word!

On our 1985 Ashes tour over here, we tried the idea of playing County matches over four days. It was an interesting experiment – which seemed to go down like a lead balloon, in the home dressing rooms! The English players just didn't seem to enjoy it at all. They seem to prefer the three-day stuff, where it's all go, go, go.

But I'd say a four-day match makes a better game of cricket. And it certainly makes a better grounding for players to play Test cricket at a later date. Blokes have more time to build their innings; groundsmen can prepare a good strip as opposed to just a result wicket which tends to happen. And the lads going in at numbers 6, 7 and 8 have the chance to score quite heavily, rather than going in and just slogging at bonus-point time.

Four-day cricket is an advantage, too, for the bowlers. They can't rely on declarations to get results – they have to bowl you out twice. So a young bowler learns to bowl positively and try to get wickets rather than bowling negatively to keep down the run rate. Remember, the latter ploy is no good when it comes to Tests. And anyway, I have always felt the game was designed as a simple one, whatever the French and Americans might think! Bowlers bowling out batsmen and batsmen playing as long an innings as possible, not throwing their wicket away after an over or two. I'm conservative, no believer in mucking about with the laws of the game too much.

Interestingly, we tried the reverse experiment in Australia. We tried to play three-day cricket and our players hated it. There were extended hours so more overs were required in a day's play. But with the three-day game, we found it very difficult to get results because that extra day is crucial in securing an outcome. And we weren't keen on the staged declaration; we were used to bowling sides out (or trying to, at least). Perhaps the blokes found they couldn't get off down to the beach so easily after a day's play to relax in the ocean! I don't know what it was, but it never caught on at home.

Whatever the arguments for or against the English system, I've been somewhat puzzled why more Australian cricketers have not opted for playing in England. I know the beer is lukewarm – but it can't be just that! Yet my advice would be to them: 'Come over – it can only enhance your knowledge of the game and make you a more complete cricketer.'

Some young Aussies tend to come over and have one or two seasons in League cricket up north. But that does not have quite the same intensity as playing County cricket. I can think of only a few guys from Australia who have joined English counties – Graham McKenzie, years ago, with Leicestershire, Jeff Thomson for a short while with Middlesex ('Thommo' got injured that season), Terry Alderman with Kent. Perhaps the odd one here and there apart from those few.

I thought about it a lot and I came up with the answer that not many of our guys were tuned in to the idea of being professional cricketers. They were semi-professional; they played their cricket during the summer and concentrated on other jobs and their families during the winter. And perhaps the Queensland cricketers couldn't tear themselves away from winter temperatures of around 26 degrees, for the uncertainties of an English summer! But seriously, only in the mid-1970s did people start to earn enough from the game in Australia to consider themselves professional cricketers. Then, they could entertain the idea of coming to England to play the game professionally.

There might be more in the future, although that will depend on the TCCB's registration allowance for overseas players. Nowadays, most counties go for a fast bowling professional and right now most of those guys seem to be coming from the West Indies. Quite right too. The Caribbean is a rich recruiting ground for young quickies of real ability.

But looking at it through purely Australian eyes, I believe that if we could somehow get the top twenty Australian cricketers playing County cricket, I think that within two or three years, Australian cricket would be a real force in the world game. Sure, I hope that happens anyway but I'm certain the English system would speed up our progress.

I base that belief on my own experience in County cricket. I have found that you have to work very hard for your runs over here, apart from in those declaration situations I mentioned. Otherwise, the standard is high; there are no easy run-making days.

Few County sides are pushovers in England. On a particular day on a certain type of wicket, any side can knock another one over. Until five or six years ago I would have said Australian domestic cricket was as strong, if not stronger. But our Sheffield Shield system has lost so many quality players that it has become diluted in strength. With so many young, inexperienced players coming on to the scene around the same time, the standard has dropped. And it was bound to. That is no criticism of the kids. But when the guys who went to South Africa come back into the system in a couple of years' time, there will be another new resurgence of strength in Australian cricket especially in our Test team.

Australian cricket has had a lot of highs and lows over the last ten or fifteen years. I should know – I've been on the rollercoaster for much of the time. Days when you want to shout to the heavens with joy, others when you could bawl your eyes out in disappointment. But that's cricket, that's life. You've got to take the rough with the smooth. And if you lose, just try harder next time.

English County cricket, however, hasn't really had any similar upheavals. So it has remained a balanced, strong breeding ground. And even in Australia, it's not all gloom by any means. I can see some good things in store for us. But I just hope one thing – that the last twelve months have given the young players a real insight into what it takes to be a good Test match cricketer.

Certainly, those young guys would see solid, seasoned professionals in action every day, if they played in England. Young bowlers would be bowling to players like Viv Richards, Graham Gooch, David Gower, Gordon Greenidge; master batsmen the lot. And our young batters would learn a thing or two from facing up to bowlers like Joel Garner, Terry Alderman, Richard Hadlee,

Derek Underwood and John Emburey. What a school to attend –
what masters to teach you!

Bruce Reid, who has basically just come out of club cricket in
Australia and is already one of our main strike bowlers in Test
cricket, is the kind of bloke I have in mind. Bruce is a big tall
left-armer from Western Australia with bags of potential and no
shortage of enthusiasm. He's got a huge future ahead of him as
long as he can stay fit.

Then there's a guy called Dennis Hickey who I was pleased to
see come over to England and get into the Glamorgan side midway
through the season. Dennis hails from Victoria and is a right-arm
quickie. A good young prospect with an excellent action. Another
Western Australian is Chris Matthews, a strong left-arm bowler
and a useful one at that. Chris would be a bit wild and wayward
at the moment but he'd learn a stack from playing in England.

We have so many good young players who have only played
half-a-dozen first-class games or so. But they're expected to take
wickets in first-class cricket and I reckon it's asking a bit much of
them so soon.

My views on English County cricket have changed since I joined
Essex and saw what it was really all about. I'm quite prepared to
admit that you hear stories and tales of the rigours of an English
season and you think: No way, A.B., not for you, mate! Think of
all that travelling. And playing seven days a week without a rest
for four and a half months. Too much. But coming here has educated me to the fact that playing year-round cricket doesn't do
you much harm, for a long while. OK, I'm ready for a rest and I'm
feeling tired mentally and physically. But you've got to bear in
mind I've had the additional pressures of leading the Australian
side and having all the worries and trials and tribulations of that,
too.

If I was a young rookie (this sounds like Dr W. G. Grace talking,
doesn't it!) I'd be bounding up the steps of the plane to England,
keen to get into County cricket for two or three years, as a vital
part of the learning process I had to go through. Another thing
about it all. If you allow it to, it can become too much mentally
because you start thinking to yourself: I'm playing too much
cricket and I'm getting stale. Cut out those thoughts and you have
no problems.

I consider I have extenuating circumstances. I'm now married
with two children, I have captained Australia and I've had years

of non-stop cricket. I've enjoyed it, too. But after years of it, you need a rest. What I'm saying is that if I was twenty-one, I'd be playing as much cricket as I could. If they played in Lapland, I'd be up there trying some!

I know for sure, that if I was sitting in an office I would be sitting down bored stiff within a week. Let alone doing it all year round. So I am and always will be grateful that I've had cricket as a career. But it is a short-lived career and you've got to make the most of it while you can. And being in England brought that point home to me. Thanks for the lesson!

As it has turned out, it wasn't too hard. With rain and one-day cricket, there was a fair bit of time sitting around doing nothing. And you got your few days off here and there which was nice. But I should add something here – it would have been impossible for me to have played in England without what my Essex mates might call the old 'trouble and strife'. The wife. I'm an enthusiastic pupil of cockney rhyming slang! Fancy a cup of Rosy Lea (tea)! I'll just use the old dog and bone (phone)! Seriously, the fact that I have got a family now and I am away from them a lot anyway, meant it was important they were with me for that time. I couldn't have come over and had another four or five months away from them.

So the experience was well worthwhile; a great part of my career. But it was a once and for all experience. I like you, I like your country – but I won't be back, not as a County player, anyway. There is no way I could spend year after year playing County cricket like so many world players.

I suspect that the many years players like Richards and Garner spent in County cricket, probably dulled their appetite for the game. They would be superhuman guys if it hadn't. I am puzzled as to why Somerset, with three world-class match winners in their side, have not done better. Finishing the 1985 season bottom of the County Championship with only one victory in twenty-four matches was incredible. But might it not be linked to the fact that Richards, Garner and Botham cannot turn on the magic all the time? It is hard producing centuries, day in, day out in all parts of the country. After all, no man is a machine even if 'Big Bird' seems to purr in to bowl with the smooth rhythm of a Porsche engine. He can be about as quick, too.

Now that's only my impression and I might be a million miles from the truth. Viv and Joel might say the complete opposite is the case. But all I can say is that if it was me and I had been here years, I think I would be like that. It would become the same old circuit, the same sort of matches, similar faces. I fear I would lose my edge.

I should make it clear I had intended to play the two seasons in County cricket. Only circumstances prevented me from doing that. When I agreed to play for Essex on a two-year deal, I knew nothing about an Australian tour of India, in September 1986. Neither did anyone else, as far as I know, because it wasn't arranged.

When that was fixed up, it changed everything. The five-week complete break I had promised myself from cricket had suddenly gone out of the window. And I was looking at non-stop cricket right through to March 1987. That's a heck of a long time to be playing the game competitively, especially at the highest level. And I feared I would lose my enthusiasm for the game if I came back here for another summer with Essex.

Cricket means everything to me; after my family, it's the most important thing in my life. But too much of anything gets you down – you start to lose the feeling that it is special. I'll be honest – I never want to lose that feeling, right to the day I quit the game. I enjoy it too much to start thinking this is a bore.

I'm not saying I would have felt that desperate had I come back for another year with Essex. Of course, I would have enjoyed the people at the county, the lads, the big games. But I doubted whether I could do myself justice if I was tired out after a long hard summer in the southern hemisphere. And to take Essex's money for another season knowing I wouldn't be at my best, was not something I was prepared to consider. For them, for me. Reputations suffer all round in that sort of situation. Besides, Ray East would have made too many rude remarks about my batting!

I wanted to play County cricket to fulfil an ambition and top off my career, because I got the taste for it in 1977. I saw what the County scene was like and enjoyed the season I had down at Gloucestershire, playing Second Eleven stuff. They were really good to me and it was a great education. And over the years you see so many great players coming to England to play County cricket, I wanted to experience what it was like.

That summer, I played club cricket for a team called Downend. It is a famous little ground there with the place where Dr W. G. Grace had his practice just across the road. Ideal for an Aussie – cricket history right on the doorstep! It was a very good introduction for me into how the County professional player goes about playing, and I was very interested in the whole County scene. It went a long way in my education for higher honours.

Something else you have to get educated about in the game is sledging . . . the use of verbals to unsettle players at the wicket. But I didn't run into that at Downend. I can't imagine much of that going on in the good Doctor's day, especially in rural Gloucestershire. More like, 'would the Doctor like me to bowl if he's ready'. 'Bowl when you wish,' a deep voice might have boomed out, from the batting crease. And so a legend was born.

To be honest, I haven't come across sledging very much at all in England. There wasn't any of that stuff in the 1985 Ashes series probably because the two teams seemed to respect each other. Sure, a bowler might make some quip at some stage or another. But that's nothing – it's the organized sledging which is the real thing. It doesn't happen really on the County circuit, either. Maybe that's because County guys don't have any sort of hatred for an opponent. It's a guy to dismiss at the other end and you are just doing your job.

Personally, I don't know that I could claim I have never gone in for it in my career. I'm not lilywhite and I'm certainly no saint! I have had my moments when I've been particularly frustrated in a game, more in Test matches for Australia. The tension is a lot greater in those circumstances and I guess everyone gets a bit excited and het up. You might say something to an opposition player and perhaps I've done that sometimes. Really, it's only about controlling your emotions better. And I don't like to see a fast bowler give it the big verbal barrage for no particular reason.

Constant harassment of a young player, especially when he first comes in with all the blokes round the bat giving him a hard time, did creep into the game a little bit. Well, Tests get important, don't they? People get keyed up. Perhaps it was inevitable. But for me, although I'm all for playing the game as hard as possible, it ought to be in the right spirit.

Maybe that has come into my attitude more in recent years whereas before, I might have a got at a player if I thought he deserved it. But I never got that involved in heated discussions with opponents. But don't call me soft – please. You'd be wrong and completely misunderstanding me. I play hard and I play to win. There are no in betweens with me. I'll play to the limit because that's often how far you have to go to win games, especially Test matches. And I'm out there rooting for Australia, no one else. So I'm not Mr Charity, no way. And I don't want to be known as such.

A few years ago, two players really got at the old sledging. Ian Chappell and Glenn Turner did not get on at all, on or off the field. The Australian captain and the New Zealand batsman simply didn't see eye to eye. They didn't like each other and they made no pretensions to the contrary. So at any opportunity they would abuse each other on the field. But in my time, Ian Chappell wasn't a sledger, as such. I know he had this reputation for it, but you speak as you find. And I seldom saw Ian getting terribly stewed up about anyone, except perhaps Turner. And in that case the feeling was quite mutual!

Ian would tend to make a smart comment, rather than an obnoxious one. If a bloke was struggling, he might walk past him and ask, dead pan face set, if his bat had a hole in it, in the middle! And we'd have a laugh at that as we walked past. But it was a smart type comment rather than giving a bloke a hard time about his parenthood being of dubious vintage! Ian was just a guy who played the game very hard and, at times, didn't get on with certain individuals. He and Tony Grieg didn't really hit it off.

It works the other way, too, because I know Keith Fletcher has mixed emotions about some of us Australians because Dennis Lillee used to give him the benefit of his thoughts a few times. And Marshie might have said some things from behind the stumps although in his case it was probably part and parcel of the game because he was also trying to gee up his fast bowlers.

But the worst bloke I ever came across for the verbals was Lennie Pascoe, our former Test fast bowler. Lennie was a scream – he would threaten to knock your block off, say he was trying to kill you and everything else! But the trouble with Lennie was that when he got into that mood, he tended to lose a bit of control because he would try and bowl faster and faster. So if you wanted to wind him up, you would say things like, 'I always thought you were supposed to be a fast bowler, Lennie. Shows how wrong you can be about a bloke...' That would do it. Lennie would growl furiously, his face would darken with fury and the obvious would happen: he would come hurtling in with the next ball and hurl the thing down at you like a man heaving a giant boulder.

Poor old Lennie – his line and length probably wouldn't be what they should have been. So you would go on to the back foot and crash him through the covers or hook him for a boundary. And that would make him even more angry. If you could keep a straight face by now, you might have another little word or two for him, something like, 'Christ, Lennie, what's happened to the quick stuff, mate? Getting tired?' And sure enough, he would bowl even faster and shorter. So you could pick even more runs off him!

Lennie could be a pretty abrasive character on the field. He was always giving you his thoughts on what sort of a player you were. And they were seldom complimentary so he could expect a bit of stick back from the batsmen when they got in the mood! In saying this, Len off the field was a great bloke and reasonably quiet (except in team meetings!). But put the ball in his hand and he became super competitive and rather vocal.

7

Marshall at Ilford: the confrontation of the season

It was time for Essex to face a bowler every bit as quick as Lennie Pascoe; someone quicker, in fact. And it's not being unkind to Lennie to say that this opponent was a more complete, all round international fast bowler. One of the best in the business, in fact, if not *the* very best. Malcolm Marshall.

If I was put right on the spot, I'd say Malcolm is the *premier* fast bowler in the world at the moment. Sure, Joel Garner might be more difficult to play because of the bounce he generates in his high action. And when you get to this level, you can't forget Michael Holding, one of the finest there has been.

Malcolm is a superb quick bowler and he deserves every ounce of respect people have for him. He is always a thoroughly difficult customer. That leaping run reminds me of a clock wound right up to its limit ... and the ticking then released. With Malcolm, it's like releasing a bomb. He's quick, he's clever and he's dangerous. And yet I was looking forward to another meeting with him.

To me, the age-old classic confrontation between a real speed merchant and a batsman is one of the joys of the game. It's the real thing; no holds barred. You are both performers at the peak of your abilities. Someone is going to come out on top and you hope like hell it isn't going to be the other guy this particular day.

I've been asked countless times about my thoughts as I face up to a fast bowler of Marshall's ability. Am I scared? Do I experience fear? Is it a worry of being seriously injured? What goes through my mind when I'm facing a speed merchant who is also a good bowler?

Well, I'm certainly not thinking what won the 3.30 at Ascot, or whether I'll have prawns or steak for dinner that night! In fact, my mind is almost totally cleared of everything except concentrating on the job in hand. With bowlers of this quality, you need all your wits about you. One moment's wavering in concentration can lose you your wicket.

If you talk to the best batsmen around the world, they would probably say very little on the subject. No one likes to admit who their really difficult opponents are, do they? But the one guy I think they'd all come up with, if you pushed them, is Marshall. And I am much the same – he is the one who conjures up the most fear.

Is it fear? No, not exactly. I think apprehensive is the best word to describe the way I feel about facing him. I'm not scared of him bowling quickly and hitting me on the head. But I'm apprehensive about him sending down some rocket well enough to get me out. That concerns me more than anything. If he hits me on the head, OK, that's part of the game. I'm not going to cry foul or anything like that.

A fast bowler has such weapons in his armoury – if you go out to face him, you accept the consequences. Anyway, if you get hit most places it's just a fleshy blow, no big deal. I suppose it's different if it is on some part of the head or the point of the elbow – that might hurt. But if not, the blow just stings for a while and you get a bruise. That's nothing to write home about, is it? If you counted up the number of cricketers who have been hit and come out with plenty of bruises after facing quick bowlers down the years, you'd have a list as long as Rodney Marsh's number of stories and jokes. And that's a few, I can tell you!

I'm not a fool – I would never say I am happy to receive a blow. but if you cop it, you damn well get on with it in my opinion. You think to yourself: He hasn't got me out. The thing about bowlers of Marshall's quality and pace is that if you give them half a sniff of victory, they'll be all over you. Like a rash. So it is imperative you hold your own. Of course, you get better with practice.

The first time I ever played against the West Indies, I couldn't believe what was happening. I felt completely out of my depth. I couldn't imagine I would ever do anything against them except just block the ball and somehow try and keep the thing out. The idea of actually thrashing them for boundaries was a joke. I thought I was going through purgatory. I'd never come across anything quite like that before,

It's the oldest story in the book, isn't it? You get accustomed to anything, and that's what happened to me. You react differently after a while. Nowadays, it seems quite usual to see the ball sailing over your head or whistling past your ears. All part of life's pleasures, eh? Well, I concede it is an awesome experience when you first experience that. And I do sometimes feel sorry for young players coming up against it for the first time. I know what they're going through.

Essex met Malcolm Marshall and Hampshire at Ilford for the first of two Championship matches on that ground. When you have played at venues like Lord's, the MCG at Melbourne and a few others, it is always interesting to find yourself at a place like Ilford. Cricket isn't all about massive grounds of international repute; remember, it goes right back to the roots. So Ilford it was and Hampshire batted first. We had them in some trouble at 130 for seven until Bobby Parks came in to join Robin Smith. They settled in and made our initial calculations start to look somewhat askew.

Robin hasn't yet played Test cricket, like his brother Chris. But then he is five years younger than Chris and is still only learning the game really. But if he can tighten his defence a little, he will be a challenge to any bowler in any form of cricket. There is no question about his positive attitude for he attacks ever so well. Maybe he is a fraction loose in defence at this time – but it is only about learning how to temper your game according to the conditions. Like I say, absorbing the learning process.

There certainly isn't any doubt that all the potential is there. His range of strokes is immense. One way and another, the Smith family took the opportunity to remind Essex of what good cricketers they are that weekend. Robin made 87 on the Saturday; Chris got an unbeaten 75 in the Sunday match. I began to wonder what was going to come on the Monday!

Chris has a lot of guts and he'll battle away for a side. Maybe he doesn't have his brother's range of shots but he is the kind of player to produce an important innings for you, in a tight situation. In other words, a valuable guy to have in your side. I thought he was unlucky to get only the one Test in 1986 for England. He came in for David Gower in the Second Test against India at Headingley. He got a few, was by no means disgraced but then found himself left out. I felt from what I could see, whoever England had picked for that match, they would have struggled to get runs on that wicket.

At Ilford, however, Hampshire recovered well to make 260. On that wicket I felt it was a decent score. And by the close, it looked even better with us standing at 37 for three – Gooch, East and Prichard all out. It was obviously going to be a battle on the Monday against Marshall.

Before that, however, Hampshire took the chance to demonstrate their fantastic strokeplay. They won the Sunday League match and won it well. Six wickets is a sizeable margin in this form of cricket. Yet when we had made 256 for five in our 39 overs, we thought we had done well. Keith Fletcher made 62, I got 75 and Gooch made 39. But so much for any thoughts of an impregnable total! Hampshire started by belting us around mercilessly. And they kept right on doing that. They reached their target with an over and a half to spare, Chris Smith and Mark Nicholas putting on an unbeaten 104 which took them to victory. Defeat for us meant Somerset, who beat Kent, caught Yorkshire and ourselves up at the top of the table. Things were hotting up.

And so to Monday ... and the best contest of the whole summer, from my point of view. Call me a masochist, if you like, but a clash with Marshall on a wicket on which, every now and then, one ball would powder and go through the top, was my idea of fun! Those balls which flew off the surface were very difficult to keep out but they certainly steeled your concentration. You never knew when one was coming so you had to be ready every ball.

It's interesting comparing the difference between a guy like Malcolm Marshall and Ian Botham. With Malcolm, the most you're likely to exchange is a knowing glance. By that I mean what I say. If he does you and beats you, you'll get the 'look'. Written all over that expression are the words: I've done you and I'm going to get you out next time. Then, if I manage to get him away a few times, I'll look up the wicket and he'll know what my expression means. There is a sort of mental telepathy between us. It's nothing vindictive or anything like that; I guess you'd call it mutual respect. And a true relish for the contest.

With Both, it's different, more of a verbal thing. He'll call you a jammy sod if you snick him for four. And I'll tell him what I thought of a ball if I've hooked him or played an authentic drive for a boundary. It's fun with Both – we both feel we have a good friendship. But there's no way that ever extends to what goes on out in the middle. People who thought our friendship in any way cost Australia the Ashes in 1985, really didn't understand how we work. I bet if you asked Both who he'd love to get out if he's playing against a side I'm in, he would say me. Not because I'm the greatest – just because our friendship seems to deepen the rivalry. It's a good feeling if you've taken a big score off a mate. You enjoy your beers even more at the end of the day's play.

Against Marshall and Hampshire on 16 June, I made 71. I did it without a helmet because I had got out of the habit of wearing one. I hadn't felt for sometime I might get hit on the head. But in the second innings, I wore one because the ball was going through the surface and taking off at times. Neil Foster got a few balls to climb and he hit Nigel Cowley (twice) and Bobby Parks in the visor, when Hampshire batted in the second innings.

I figured that if Foster could do that, Marshall might actually knock your block off with a real quick one on that wicket! But the psycho-analysis of that situation would fascinate the experts. What do you do? If you wear a helmet maybe the bowler thinks you're conceding something before you start. But if you don't, maybe he'll think: This guy is a wise guy, a cocky what-name. I'll show him.

It's no good asking me for the correct path to steer in such a situation. After all, I'm no head shrinker! All I feel is that if you think there's any likelihood of being hit on the head, you ought to wear a helmet because they're perfectly comfortable. And that is just a straightforward precaution, like wearing thick gloves when you ski so you don't get frostbitten fingers. Plain common sense really.

Now arguments about the use of helmets are liable to stir up a hornet's nest. I've heard the old-time experts saying things like: Of course, they never used them in Don Bradman's day. It must mean today's players are technically inferior. Well I dispute that view. Sure, you never saw the Don in one. Half of England would have come to a grinding halt through shock if he'd walked out at Lord's wearing one, in 1948! 'I say, what on earth is the chap up to', sort of cry . . . !

Anyone can watch the old films from the cricket archives. And they all show that nothing like as many short-pitched balls were bowled in those days. I've sat glued to the video machine for hours studying the 'Bodyline' series. And people seemed to go into absolute pandemonium when batsmen got hit in the ribs.

But times change, don't they? People went into raptures when the first four-minute mile was run. Nowadays, a guy like the New Zealander John Walker has beaten the four-minute barrier for the mile, over 100 times! And when Steve Cram *only* records a time of 3.50.12 for the mile, people seem disappointed! In the Bodyline series, crowds were in uproar at the Adelaide Test when Bert Oldfield tried to hook one and got hit on the top of the head. But such things seem fairly common in this day and age. The West Indies have four pace bowlers who see nothing unusual in hitting a batsman. And I don't query their attitude in the slightest because if Australia had four bowlers of that quality, we would be doing exactly the same thing. And so would England.

It's up to the batsmen to come to terms with the short, rising ball. Certainly on uneven pitches you have no chance against that stuff. England experienced that in the West Indies in 1986. But play those guys on a wicket like the one we had in Sydney for the last Test against the West Indies in 1985, and you blunt their fast bowling to a certain extent.

But even if the West Indies' attack is quick and nasty, I don't believe in penalizing them for having those attributes. I reckon you've got to stand up to it, that's all. And maybe that is what has been lacking recently against them. After all, you've got to be prepared to get in there and cop a few to get a few. Who was it who said something about staying out of the kitchen, if you couldn't stand the heat ... ?

Personally, I don't envy the quick bowlers these days. Rushing in bowling fast is not my idea of lighthearted relaxation. If you stand up to them for a couple of hours and grit your teeth, it's amazing how the runs do start to come. So get stuck in is my philosophy. And don't bleat about it, mate!

By the end of that Monday, the bowlers had certainly proved a point at Ilford. Nineteen wickets fell that day, with Essex all out for 198 giving Hampshire a lead of 62. That was about, well, 62 runs too many on that wicket! But our guys fought back well with the ball to dismiss Hampshire for 135 in their second innings. So we wanted 198 for victory. If that looked difficult considering the prevailing conditions, then the loss of Gooch and Prichard for 27 by the close, made it start to look as easy a job as scampering up K2 mountain in Nepal! By the most difficult route. But Essex grit, although it might not resemble Clint Eastwood's style, thrives. And at 156 for five next day, we were thriving all right. Only 42 needed. There was probably just one last obstacle to a tremendous Essex win ... yep, you've named him, Malcolm Marshall.

It had been a game of changing fortunes. First we'd do well, then Hampshire would come right back at us. Nip and tuck. Good cricket. Highly competitive, too. Marshall, we figured, must be getting tired. He had bowled a long spell, surely he couldn't go on for ever. And if he was withdrawn from the attack, I think the psychological lift would have propelled us to victory.

I drove Malcolm for four to reach 54. Derek Pringle and Alan Lilley had played vital parts. Then, without many dramas going on at the other end, 'Bandit' gave me a brute of a ball. Hours later I was still trying to analyse how I could have avoided it. The answer, apart from running away to square leg which I'm not in the habit of doing, was ... I couldn't! He had brought the ball into me frequently, with an area just about on my middle stump from which the odd ball was kicking into my ribs and gloves down the legside. I'd had a few knocks, but the pain had been eased by the sight of the scoreboard ticking along closer to 198. Great antidote to any pain, a moving scoreboard! Then this ball hit the pitch and exploded like a grenade. It struck my glove and went straight up in the air. In such a situation, there is always that brief moment before it falls into a hand. Long enough for you to realize what has happened. Oh no, oh hell, is a popular thought in most batsmen's minds, I guess.

Our tail-enders did put up a good fight. Neil Foster smacked a few and Charlie Childs stood it for a while, which was another good effort after his 30 in the first innings. So it got down to two good hits ... twelve runs to win. At which stage our last wicket fell. We were out for 185 and had lost.

It was the sort of game I had expected County cricket to be: close, good contests rather than the kind of matches 'set up' by declarations. Not a thing was given away by any player in this game. And that suited me.

Ilford is basically a park ground and the fact that the grounds-man only ever really prepared it for one-day fixtures, was illustrated by the wickets we had that week. The one we had for the Sunday fixture was excellent but I didn't think the others were good enough. In both matches, against Hampshire and Sussex, the wicket played all right for a day and a half but then started to play up. That was probably because the surface didn't have the right top soil or preparation. In the Hampshire match, they got it completely wrong because the surface 'went' very early on. It seemed well below par for what you would expect; not really good enough for first-class cricket. The wicket for the Sussex match threatened to become bad but never did. With the passage of time, and the ball getting older, it became easier to bat. Which is what happens, of course, in any normal match.

It came down to the fact that winning the toss was a huge advantage. You could bat first and avoid batting last when it was very unpredictable. Maybe if we had played Hampshire on a better wicket, the luck factor would not have been quite so important. But against that view, others would claim that those wickets provided for two good 'results' in the week. And they would be right. So it boils down to what you want – good, true wickets which last and therefore probably require some 'manipulation' to produce a result. Or a wicket which breaks up and ensures a result. Two different schools of thought – and it's not easy to say which is exactly right.

There was definitely one advantage of playing on that type of wicket – it provided an excellent chance to assess wicketkeepers. The 'keeper who can take the ball consistently cleanly on a difficult track where the ball is climbing or turning a fair amount, stands out as a quality performer. A ball popping, leaping or shooting makes a 'keeper's life tough. And Hampshire's Bobby Parks handled those conditions very well. He seemed well organized, took the ball cleanly and did the job very effectively. When I saw England had asked him to go to Lord's to stand in for the injured Bruce French on the Saturday of the First Test against New Zealand, I reckoned a selector or two must have been peeping through the hedge at Ilford! Parks was impressive that day.

Overall, it looks as if there is not much between the top four or five 'keepers in England at present. French, Richards, Parks, Rhodes, East ... they all seem to be roughly the same in terms of ability.

Judging wicketkeepers and their true value is hard for anyone like me who saw two of the best there have ever been in his formative years. Most guys standing back are basically on a par with the best but it's on the turning wickets that you sort out your quality men. Occasionally you get freaks like Alan Knott who don't miss a thing, anywhere.

I'd have to say I don't see any Knottys around these days. That guy was, dare I say it, probably the best wicketkeeper there has ever been. I just cannot remember him letting England down and amazingly, he used to score runs in that situation as well, when the side needed them. That made him, in my mind, the best the world has seen.

I played a lot of cricket with Rod Marsh and I'd say Rod was only a fraction behind Alan. Although I know it's unfair to compare, I always have those two in my mind when I look at other young 'keepers. It's like anything – you go and look at a painting by Rembrandt and the piece of work you're offered by an artist at the local arts and crafts fair, doesn't really compare. Of course, it's silly to put them side by side – but maybe it's human nature to do that.

Our wicketkeeper at Essex, David East, is what you might call awkward-looking because he's a left-handed 'keeper. So he has to catch the ball and throw it back left-handed, something which some people don't think looks good. OK, it might not be as pretty as a right-hander, but 'Eastie' has done a fantastic job for most of the season. He stands up at the stumps to the medium pacers, and he can also bat. A useful guy. Bobby Parks is probably a better looking wicketkeeper than East but there would not be much between them in terms of ability.

The situation here in England is about the same as ours in Australia, in that department. We've got a young fellow who may come through, long term, on the Australian scene. His name is Greg Dyer and he's from Sydney. As he plays at the SCG, with its spinners' wicket, he tends to keep up at the stumps quite a bit which is useful experience. On our one-day campaigns in New Zealand, in 1986, Tim Zoehrer was the guy in the position. But Tim might do well to improve his attitude to the game. There is the suspicion that he doesn't do enough work in practice. The 'greats' I've watched like Knott and Marsh both worked a great deal on their skills. I sometimes used to think Knotty was paranoic about it. But look at the 'keeper he was; that answered such thoughts. And he kept himself so superbly fit he could take catches anywhere. He could probably have earned a gold medal in the Olympics for diving, he did so much of it on the cricket field! Whatever it took for Knott and Marsh to make sure when they got into a game they didn't miss a thing, they did it.

Tim Zoehrer seems to slacken off to a certain extent. He has been given a fantastic opportunity, keeping wicket for his country, and I'd like to see him doing a little more work. But Greg Dyer is a good enough batsman to force his way into the Test team as just a batter, so over the next couple of years it should be interesting to see the outcome. One thing's for sure – if either bloke has half the character of Rod Marsh, the guys in the Aussie sides will have some laughs in the coming years. How that guy inspired his team-mates, day in, day out.

Against Sussex, our next opponents at Ilford, we won the toss. Our first good move. But we made only 242, which wasn't really enough to make us start sending out for the jeroboams of champagne! I wasn't too special, either; out, bowled Reeve, 17. But Prichard, Fletcher and Foster all made half centuries.

You couldn't say the course of our innings was exactly smooth. We were 22 for two, recovered to 149 for four, then slipped to 167 for six and made 242. But anyone who thought there had been a few dramas in that innings, hadn't seen anything. It was like the calm before the storm, when Sussex batted.

We had fourteen overs to bowl at them on the first night. In that situation, you hope for as many wickets as possible. But I suppose you'd have to say 30 for two or 30 for three was about the best you'd expect. Anything else and you'd think Christmas had come early. Well, we had Christmas and Easter rolled into one that night. Sussex closed at 16 for six. I'd never experienced anything like it in my life before. Every good ball got a wicket, every little snick went to hand. We even had a run-out in that lot. Sussex were staggering like drunks at a close of tour party! We sure enjoyed a beer that night.

We'd even done that without John Lever, who had been called up by England. Don Topley took his place and on his first Championship appearance of the season took four wickets for seven runs, in seven overs. We thought we might see pigs flying across the sky over the pavilion if we looked up! But ... we hadn't got Imran that night. And he made 49 the next morning, steering Sussex away from the danger of a follow-on, like a wise old sea dog at the wheel in a heavy storm. They made 112. Then, in our second innings, there came another incident that was to cause a few raised eyebrows around the county circuit. This match seemed to be full of incidents!

When we batted again, we had a lead of 130. You didn't need

to be a University graduate to understand we needed quick runs to get Sussex in chasing as big a target as possible. Things went well for us, too – Prichard made 55, Keith Pont 31. Then I got among the runs, during which time I got a message that we were going to declare at 5.50. Fletch wanted to have a go at Sussex that night and as it was 5.20 when I got the message, I started to have a go. I'd made about 50 by then and as the clock ticked towards 5.50, I began to get very close to 100. But when Fletch came out to bat for the last couple of overs, I told him straightaway: 'Don't worry about me or my hundred. Declare at 5.50 to get half an hour at them.' Even so, when I was on 95, Colin Wells bowled me such a long-hop I should have hit it out of the ground. I'd already hit him out of the ground for six but only swung this one down to fine leg and couldn't get back for two. So Fletch was on strike for the last ball and I was left 96 not out when he declared.

It didn't bother me in the slightest. The way I saw it, we wanted to get a wicket or two that night. We had enough runs in the bank. Nothing else mattered. If you become the sort of cricketer who worries only about your own scores and achievement, you're missing the whole idea of what is, after all, a team game. Anyway, you ought to be in computers or accountancy if figures are the only things that interest you! I didn't give it another thought, especially as we got two Sussex wickets that night, one in the very last over. That justified Fletch's decision to declare when he did.

The next morning, to my surprise, the papers seemed to make all sorts of sensations out of it. There were headlines like: 'Essex declare with Border 96 not out'. Frankly, I couldn't see what all the fuss was about. And I certainly didn't have it in mind to take up the issue with Fletch, clutching a meat cleaver in my hands! Some of the papers seemed to suggest I ought to be pretty upset. A lot of rubbish. If I'd batted on for just one more ball to make a century, we wouldn't have got that second wicket that night. And even then, we didn't get the last wicket in the match until the final half a dozen overs. Point proven, in my book. We set Sussex 360 and they fought well to reach 290. I was happy – we won the match. What else mattered?

I like the Essex attitude to such matters. They regard the team situation as the only criterion. That's fine by me. And I reckon it goes a long way to explain why they have been so successful in recent years. You win trophies with that sort of attitude.

Imran Khan didn't trouble us as much as Malcolm Marshall had done at Ilford. But then the wicket played better in the Sussex match and blunted 'Immie'. But despite that, the guy is quick, very quick when he wants to be. I've sometimes faced him and found it hard to see much difference in pace between himself and Marshall. I don't think there is a better bowler with an old ball than Immie; even on the flattest of wickets, he's still able to move the old ball around. That ability to curl the ball around puts you off your game a bit. You're never sure about a ball, what it's going to do. Immie strikes me as a wily old fox. He's thirty-four but still in the top half dozen bowlers in the world.

I'd made a few runs at Ilford that week – 71, 54, 17 and 96 not out. But taking the season overall to that stage, I felt I'd been a shade hit and miss. Exactly that really – hitting well some days, missing out on others! And the next match showed just what I meant, although I wasn't exactly going out of my way to try and demonstrate any failings!

The pitch was very lively for our game against Middlesex at Lord's. We took a good close look at it so when we won the toss, we put Middlesex in. You wonder when you do that, to start with anyway. But we didn't have many worries with Middlesex at 66 for five. But Roland Butcher, with 86, and Mike Roseberry, a youngster who got 36, pulled Middlesex round so that they finished on a total of 208. But we had them out quickly, in 68.3 overs. Don Topley, who seemed as though he only had to reach the bowling crease and turn his arm over to take wickets in this purple patch, took four. Keith Pont also got four victims.

Middlesex had problems with the ball 'flying' at times. When we batted, Wayne Daniel and Norman Cowans arranged a very spicy reception committee for us! At 76 for seven we were in severe trouble, before Neil Foster's 36 not out pushed us to 109 for seven by close on that Saturday. Seventeen wickets had fallen in the day at Lord's; enough to send the older members scurrying away to the bar for a large brandy and soda to revive themselves. It was a bit of a shock to us, too!

I didn't bat for long. Some of the newspaper reports the next day were not all that kind about my shot. But I don't think they can have been watching the same game. It was made out to be a wild swish which ended up with my middle stump being knocked out. But I saw it as a ball from Cowans of pullable height. Except that it came through at chest height and when I tried to pull it, I got an edge and the ball was diverted on to my stumps off the bottom of the bat. OK, it wasn't a masterful stroke to be playing first ball after tea, in our precarious position. But I'm not sure it justified the inference that I ought to be hanged, drawn and quartered!

The Middlesex bowling was good and there was some sharp catching. The wicket helped explain the slump a little ... but not entirely. Sorry, lads, I can't blame it on the pitch this time! It seemed like poor batting had contributed to such low scoring rather than the wicket playing any major tricks.

It was a good hard, fast track which offered the bowlers a little assistance. If fast bowlers get pace and bounce out of tracks, that's really what they want. And Middlesex certainly had us out quickly on the Monday, after only seven more overs, for 130. A result was inevitable – especially by lunch that day when Middlesex dined uneasily at 67 for eight. Only Paul Downton with 36 could have enjoyed his meal. Middlesex crashed for 97, leaving us 176 to win. But ... the seamers were getting a fair bit of movement and the bounce had become irregular.

I looked at what had happened and I was puzzled. All those wickets, thirty, for only 435 runs. Maths was never my great strength but even I could see each batsman's average was no more than 15. And I couldn't understand it. There was the feeling in my mind that you could score runs on the pitch. It didn't have to be just survival. Yet statistics proved otherwise. That night, when we closed at 29 for one, I felt I could get runs the next day.

I fancied my chances because the way I figured it, batting was all about playing straight, leaving the wide ones alone and working out where you should be scoring. If you followed those ground rules, it seemed anyone could make runs. Perhaps English County players were not used to a wicket which offered pace and bounce. But I was – I'd grown up on similar surfaces back home. And I didn't intend to miss out here.

Paul Prichard (35) and Alan Lilley (36) rather proved the point. And with 59 not out, I was there when we won the match. But it had been a good test. Whether it was the occasion or the wicket I'm not sure but Wayne Daniel certainly let them go with genuine pace in both innings. He would probably be no higher than about eighth in line in the West Indies Test match selection process for fast bowling. But I'll bet England wish he was available to them and I reckon we would use him, too, if he had Australian parents or something! When Wayne has his rhythm right, he's as quick as all of them.

Norman Cowans, at the other end, concentrated on bowling a good line and length and, if the ball was going to take off, let it do so itself. For hours he sent down more, what we call in the trade wicket-taking balls, in that match than many I'd seen for ages.

The thought has been voiced that Norman has failed because he never became the strike bowler England were looking for. But that's harsh on him. I get on well with Norman, I like him. We have talked a fair amount. It's clear that he's trying to become a bowler who bowls six dot balls; that is, every one on the spot. And if the wicket is doing something to help him, let the ball do it by putting it in the right place.

Norman hasn't got explosive pace, but as he showed against us (five for 61 in the first innings) he's a mighty useful performer. He's attempting to acquire the art of bowling long spells without giving much away. And if he masters that, who is to say he won't play for England again?

From England's point of view, it has to be a pity that Roland Butcher hasn't played Test cricket since 1981. A pity for you but not for us. The guy is a magnificent fielder and batting with someone like that prowling around the covers like some cat, is not easy, I can tell you. You begin to wonder if you'll ever get a run close to him.

'Butch' hit the ball well against us to make 86. But he must have been disappointed not to make a big hundred and shut us right out of the game. Having got so far, he would have wanted to go on and certainly avoid the sort of loose shot which got him out. But playing like that has always been his trait. And if you play your cricket like that, you live and die. There don't seem to be any in betweens for Butch.

Middlesex, the defending Champions, had played Essex, the current Championship leaders, with quality players like Edmonds, Emburey, Gatting, Gooch, Pringle, etc. out of the match, due to Test match duties. That was a pity. You'd have to be honest and admit their absence detracted from the game. At full strength, it would have been a terrific contest. Without those guys, maybe it was like Punch and Judy, without the two leading figures!

But the contrary view is that it's good to see both sides developing Test match cricketers, because that should be the aim of all Counties. I do think the reserve strength on display at Lord's for this match showed that these teams were among the best in the country, whatever the current Championship table might say.

Since 1979, Middlesex and Essex have, between them, won fifteen of the 29 trophies available in domestic cricket. Not a bad statistic, is it, if you live anywhere near Lord's or Chelmsford? Those supporters have had some great years to cheer. But cricket is like life; all glory is fleeting. As long as those fans remember that, no worries. Good times do end, yes, even if you're West Indian. Honestly, I do believe that.

8

Lord's and Jesmond: bats apart

Lord's was deserted, just a few isolated spectators sitting around the ground in clusters, huddling under umbrellas. It was the sort of scene which folk who either don't understand cricket or have no special affinity towards the game, simply cannot begin to contemplate. Deriving pleasure from sitting in an almost empty ground, maybe in rain, just waiting for a lot of guys to come out and hit a ball around.

My admiration for people who sit there in such conditions knows no bounds. They're the lifeblood of the game, in my book; the real fans. Without people as keen as that, cricket all over the world would be struggling. Thank God for cricket nuts and fanatics, I say, in the nicest possible way.

For a few minutes, it didn't seem to matter to me that the rain was coming down more and more heavily. I allowed my thoughts to be seduced by the intoxicating atmosphere of Lord's; *the* great cricket ground in the world. Lord's, the home of cricket. Lord's, where England had fought Australia for the Ashes. Lord's, the great ground from where I had heard so many Test matches played out over the years. It was a poignant moment for me, rich in nostalgia and memory.

I'm not usually one for too much looking back. I face cricket the way I face life; eager for the next challenge. But the timelessness of Lord's Cricket Ground seems to infect everyone. And I'm not ashamed to admit, it's a great feeling to be inside that marvellous sporting arena. Whenever I come to England, I go to Lord's and make a point of sitting and looking at the famous view from the pavilion. It means so much to me.

Years ago, when I was just a kid, I'd crawl out of bed early in the morning back home in Sydney, turn on the radio and listen to the live broadcast from the Test match in England, against Australia. Lord's was always my favourite ground. The word seemed to conjure up all sorts of dreams and images. In those days, I probably thought I'd never even see the place, let alone play cricket there. Certainly not for my country. I remember the first time I saw the ground I was amazed at the slope. In Australia, we don't have that sort of thing; all our grounds are very level. In those radio broadcasts of the Test matches, the commentators had talked about the slope and the Lord's ridge. I hadn't imagined what they were on about! Being an Australian, you don't realize until you come to the ground, the amount it does drop.

Even when you play at Lord's in a County match rather than a Test, there is still something special about walking out on to the ground in your whites. I think I must be becoming an old romantic, in my advanced years!

I first saw Lord's in 1977. I was down in Bristol playing Second Eleven cricket with Gloucestershire and I got tickets from Richie Benaud, an old friend, to come up for the Lord's Test. Imagine the excitement – I was like a five-year-old with a new choc bar for the day!

Over the years I've heard people complain about the size of Lord's. They say it's too short on the sides, etc. But for me, as far as a cricket spectacle is concerned, it's great because the stands are very close to the action. You see the ball crashing into the fence for four: you see the fielders chasing the ball.

How does Lord's compare with other grounds? Well, I don't particularly like the MCG in Melbourne; it's too vast for a cricket ground, to my way of thinking. However, you do get some fantastic support there (not if you're a Pom!). Walk out on to that arena as an Australian cricketer in front of 75,000 fans and you get a real buzz of support! And when the Aussies are doing well, it's tremendous.

I much prefer Sydney as a ground but coming back to England, I also like Old Trafford, Manchester. I have good memories as an Australian player there (Botham excepted!) and I like the Lancastrian crowds, too. They give us a bit of razz as Australians but they're pretty fair, and good knowledgeable cricket people. I spent some time playing in the Lancashire League and I found the people very warm and friendly.

Headingley, as a ground, I loathe; I think it's terrible. But I'd have to say I've been influenced in that view by events over the years as an Australian player. Botham's spectacular innings and England's astonishing victory up there in 1981, when they looked like losing by an innings, didn't help my thought process. But that wasn't the only example.

In 1983 when we played the West Indians there, in the World Cup, we got absolutely mangled. And by the time we went back in 1985, I was fearing the worst if the form book was anything to go by. Sadly for us, it was. We lost the First Test against England!

Headingley's a ground where I've got a pretty bad sort of record, too, in a personal sense. I'd say a lot of the problems come down to the wicket. I've never ever played on a good wicket there. Or what I'd term a good wicket, anyway. It doesn't seem to offer bowlers and batsmen the same equal chance to do well. Generally wickets there are weighted too much in favour of the bowlers, although I suppose the 1985 Ashes Test didn't follow that pattern. But those high totals were freakish and the bowling wasn't very good in that match. Good medium pace or fast bowling on that ground will always lead to low scores. But then, a bowler would probably say he liked it, and I'd understand his thinking if he did. But as a batter, it's not my favourite by a long streak.

Up at Sheffield earlier in the 1986 season, I was copping a certain amount of razz because it looked like Yorkshire were going to win the Sunday League game quite easily. I was fielding down at the fence and got a bit of lip. Whether it's meant to be good-natured or not you never know. But I can't say it's one of the pleasures of life being called 'kangaroo' or 'convict'. It's all fairly basic stuff. But overall, I think I've been treated very well in England. I do expect to get a bit of stick on the boundary and it doesn't bother me because if an Englishman came out and played in Australia, I know what he could expect. And I don't mean he'd be called a 'jolly nice sort of chap from the old country'. Not quite, anyway!

Lord's . . . now there's a place to invoke some good old memories for me, when I'm a doddering old boy in Brisbane with a grandchild on my knee! Poor child – I'll probably bore him or her half to distraction with stories from the famous Lord's Cricket Ground.

Well actually I hope I won't become like that. But then, you never quite know how senility is going to catch you, do you?

I look back now on that 1985 innings, in the Second Test at Lord's, as the best I've ever played in international cricket. Things were not exactly going our way prior to that innings. We'd lost the First Test at Headingley and I'd taken the gamble of putting England in at Lord's, after I'd won the toss. They say Australians love a gamble and I'd had one that morning, all right. It's always a gamble to send the opposition in but I felt our best chance of winning with the way the wicket was, lay in fielding first. The outfield was quite sluggish and I felt that if we could get a good start with the ball, we'd have an advantage in batting on the second and third days – probably the best time to bat in the match, I guessed.

We did bowl well and had England out for 290 on the second morning. So far, so good. But 101 for four wasn't what we'd had in mind for our innings. I told Greg Ritchie that, too, when we came together. I felt in good nick; there was that little feeling somewhere within which told me I might make some. And I started to hit the ball well. It kept going through my mind that I was in good form and it was up to me to stay there. I knew that if I got out we'd be under pressure because we'd have to bat last on the wicket. And doing that when you're chasing a sizeable total is never easy. I had got us into the position anyway by inserting England – it was up to me to get us well out of any trouble. So I restrained myself, attacking when I could but being careful. When I got to 196 I had visions of a double century at Lord's. Strike up the old romantic chords, again!

Both, however, had other ideas. I had made 200 once in a Sheffield Shield game but when you remember all the great players, they've all made their double centuries in Test matches. I hadn't and I wanted one this time. But Both had me, four short of the double century. And that was a big disappointment to me. Was I being too greedy? I don't believe so. You ought to set yourself the highest possible targets. Second best isn't something I'm happy to settle for. And when I got out, there was that handshake with Both. Cripes, the flak that stirred up . . .

When I got back to Australia, people said we were too chummy with the opposition and that was one of the contributory factors in our defeat in the series. They said that Both pulled the wool over our eyes, in that whilst being very friendly towards us, he was knocking us over at the same time. They said our friendliness towards him was detracting from our performances.

To all that, I said then and still say, rubbish! We were just outplayed by a better side. That's why we lost the series. Victory has nothing to do with being ultra-aggressive towards the opposition. I've been through both experiences, seen both attitudes; the abrasive approach and the friendly stuff. And from what I've seen, the cricket doesn't change at all. If you're being outplayed, you're being outplayed. Hard luck but fact. Being bloody aggressive off the field won't alter it.

In Australia, people looked for excuses as to why we lost. And because they'd seen the games played in the right spirit with players from both sides acknowledging it if someone from the other lot happened to do well, some pointed the finger at that. Wrongly, in my view. We all tried our damnedest in that series. The Australian dressing room wasn't full of namby-pambies. No way. Our guys tried their utmost and fought hard. They wanted to win, make no mistake. And the fact that I was upset when I got out for 196 at Lord's, handshake or no with Both, proved the point. You don't worry about that if you're not keyed into fighting as hard as possible for victory.

Sometimes I might consider scoring a hundred against the West Indies a greater achievement than that 196. I once made 98 not out against the West Indians at Trinidad and that day, I felt I came to terms with just about everything they could throw at me on a wicket which suited them. We ended up saving that particular game and I also got a hundred in the second innings. But when I think of Lord's and the context of the game in that it was so important a contest, I'd lean towards that innings as my best ever.

Cricket flows on, from Test to Test, County game to Minor County match. Lord's on Tuesday; Jesmond on Wednesday. A County Championship match against the champion side, followed by a NatWest Bank Trophy first round match against Northumberland. You couldn't say we weren't getting enough variety in our schedule. Why, even the method of transport was different this time. No, Concorde wasn't waiting in North London to whisk us up to the North East in fifteen minutes or something similar! But we left our cars at Lord's and caught the train that Tuesday evening. The County felt it was a long journey by road and the train would make a pleasant change. It was a view I shared. When you all travel together, it does wonders for the team spirit and morale. Especially when you've just knocked over the champion County. You get the chance, on a train, to talk among yourselves, swap jokes and discuss things: much better than all travelling in different cars.

The Jesmond ground is in the suburbs of Newcastle; a tree-lined, postage-stamp sized ground tucked away in a leafy residential road: poles apart from Lord's but still with a particular charm of its own. It is cricket at its best; back at its roots, in humble but convivial surroundings. There is a special atmosphere about the ground of course; the cricket is played in a different way. But it adds up to the same thing – a desire to play well and win. That attitude you'll find the world over.

Call me daft, if you like, but I always worry about games such as these. That's because there is only one way to go – down. You're expected to win and win easily. And when you go out to bat, people just assume you'll make runs. Find me a batsman in the world who likes that situation and I'll be surprised.

I've played so much cricket that this sort of game holds a whole different kind of excitement for me. I like playing on grounds like the one at Jesmond and in matches of this kind. Coming to the North East is interesting because I suppose it's a bit more famous for football than cricket. That seems to be the local religion on Tyneside!

Even on the day we arrived at the ground, the locals were soon buzzing with football news. Newcastle United had got Liverpool in the opening game of the new season, 23 August, at St James's Park. And that caused a great debate around the ground. You didn't have to be far-sighted to see why football has such a cult following in these parts.

The people are very hospitable. But regardless of that, we knew their charity wouldn't extend to the cricket pitch. The fact that we, like all the first-class Counties in the first round of the Trophy facing Minor County opposition, were expected to win, meant it was never going to be exactly a rest. But it was nice to get a break from the first-class County scene and have a brief look at another part of England. You know how they play their cricket in places like Canterbury, Southampton, Leicester and Bristol. It's good to see how they get on somewhere else.

A couple of large trees dominate the Jesmond ground. I reckoned they would be natural targets for some of the guys trying to hit sixes during the match. At one end of the ground, behind the wickets, there is a white stone wall with a lovely row of trees behind it. The pavilion reminded me of the one at Chelmsford – an upper tier for players with wooden slats down the front. I could imagine the locals turning up to watch Minor Counties cricket with just a small crowd of real fans, settling down into deck-chairs and enjoying a quiet afternoon's cricket. Magnificent! Cricket isn't just about Test matches and pressure games. Remember all the thousands of guys who play the game and never come near Test matches or even County standard. But the enthusiasm is not in doubt.

The NatWest competition, as the successor to the Gillette Cup (which was the original one-day knock-out cricket tournament in England), had a special meaning for me, and I was looking forward to my first game in the competition. I wasn't to be disappointed in terms of interest. I suppose some people might turn up expecting to see the County batsmen hitting every other ball out of the ground. But it doesn't work out like that. Certainly, things were not at all straightforward for us in the morning. We won the toss and batted, but the ball seamed around a bit off the wicket and Northumberland's bowlers did well. 'Chilly' Old (Chris Old formerly of Yorkshire and England!) is an old hand at wobbling the ball about and he had good support from others. Gladwin and Prichard were out early on and Gooch was just starting to break loose after a long patient spell, when he was bowled for 44.

The way the ball was finding the middle of my bat, I felt on for a good score. But the local bowling had a lot more going for it than just enthusiasm; there was some quality there as well. And I had no complaints about my dismissal. I'd made 23 and was going well when Peter Graham, a cousin of the fast bowler Norman Graham who used to play for Kent, bowled me a beauty. I had to play at it but it left me a little off the seam and bounced a bit higher than usual. I nicked it and the 'keeper took the catch.

Under those circumstances, I was not upset. How can you be? You have to accept at times that you've been done by a very good ball. There's no disgrace in that. You try and think of ways you might have played it differently. But it was just good bowling. I'd had a possible 37 overs to bat when I got in so there was time to build up a good score. But that's cricket; time and again just when you think you're set to make a lot, you get out. It's a great leveller!

The chap who got me out, Peter Graham, looked perfectly capable of playing County cricket very successfully. In fact, I'm a bit surprised he's not with a first-class County. Maybe he doesn't want to play cricket seven days a week, maybe he's got a good job outside the game. I don't know. But certainly on his performance against us – 12 overs, 3 maidens, 28 runs, 2 wickets – he's got the ability to succeed in most company. All our fellows had a lot of respect for him. He bowls seamers, goes away from the right-handers and is very accurate. Can't ask for much more, can you? He'd be a good catch for any County. Putting the ball on the spot six times out of six isn't an easy thing to do. Graham did that most of the time and he impressed me.

I knew Jesmond because I'd played up there in 1984, in the Callers Pegasus matches. It was the year Seve Ballesteros won the Open Golf Championship at St Andrews. Remember that mar-vellous TV shot of Seve, on an emotional high, adrenalin pumping, raising his fist as he sank a long putt; the decisive moment? I was there, as they say, and I enjoyed it immensely. Greg Chappell and myself were in England on a cricket-cum-golf trip, courtesy of the Callers. We played two matches, or at least we were supposed to. But the weather intervened and one was washed out. But I think that was about the only rain we saw on that whole trip. Trust cricket's luck to catch it!

Typically, as soon as the cricket was over and we headed up to Scotland for the Open, the weather changed and was glorious for the rest of the trip. It has been more than once in my life that I've thought God certainly wasn't a cricketing gent! Up in Scotland, we either watched the golf at St Andrews or played ourselves, on the magnificent Gleneagles course. A tough trip, I can tell you! We had a real ball.

Thinking back to that game at Jesmond, I had never played cricket with Barry Richards, the South African who used to play for Hampshire. But he was playing in that game. I'd seen Barry play in Australia in 1970 and he had a remarkable season, scoring over 1,000 runs and playing magnificently. You couldn't find many better textbook players to watch if you scoured the world.

I remember seeing him in Sydney on a day when he got about 170. World-class bowlers were being smashed all over the ground by this guy. The harder they tried, the stronger his strokeplay became. What a joy to watch. Then, some fourteen years later, I was actually playing with him in the unlikely surroundings of Jesmond and that in itself was a big thrill for me. Watching just how casual Barry was about the whole thing, was pretty interesting, too. Talk about laid back – he must have been the guy who invented the phrase. Oh, and while he was so laid back and low keyed, he'd be taking a century off you. That's talent for you. No, wrong word. Genius.

Barry had been retired for a couple of years and hadn't picked up a bat for twelve months before he went out to bat at Jesmond. But he just collected this new bat as he strode out to open the innings, coolness personified. It was the classic showdown. Young, fast, enthusiastic local quickie keen to make a name for himself, meets the old maestro, who had enjoyed a great reputation. A sort of wild West showdown. The first ball came down, fast and short. Barry stood there, leant back and flicked it behind square for four, without any effort. It was as if he were twenty-one, playing his first innings in County cricket.

Barry Richards made about 60 that day and I had the pleasure of batting with him at one stage. All too briefly. But it will always remain a special memory for me. The guy was so good it was a tragedy he didn't get the chance to prove it at the highest level. A lot of people say that if Barry had played for a normal period of time in Test cricket, he would have broken all sorts of records. And I'm not about to argue that point. He would conceivably have been, well maybe not Bradmanesque, but nearly up to that class. And you can't find much higher praise than that floating around.

Sadly for Barry, he played too much County cricket, day in, day out stuff and virtually no Test cricket. It was all bread and butter; no jam on it. And after a while it all became a bit humdrum for a guy with that class and he became jaded. He had nothing more to prove, nothing left to give. And he just faded away . . . one of the greatest disappointments there can have been. But probably not to him. Barry took things very placidly from what I could see. Either he made 180 quite brilliantly or he made none. If he got out, so what? There was always the next day, another innings. But genius shouldn't have to exist that way, should it? It ought to be nursed and cared for. Barry became a bit cynical about the game and just too casual. But if he'd had the excitement of being a Test cricketer, too, I think we would have seen one of the best ever.

I'd have gone an awful long way to see that opening partnership for Hampshire of Barry Richards and Gordon Greenidge. On certain days if both of them were in the mood, they must have been an awesome sight. Both would have been trying to outdo each other and you can only lick your lips at some of the strokeplay there would have been to watch.

There was some good strokeplay, too, in the latter part of our innings at Jesmond, this time. Alan Lilley provided most of it, making 113 and helping push the score up to 298 for nine off 60 overs. It left Northumberland with a mighty task.

They fought well, the Northumberland openers putting on 118 for the first wicket. But they took 39 overs to do so and after that, they never had enough time to reach our score. But 219 for five was a worthy effort against a strong County side like ours. I thought they acquitted themselves well, in the field with the ball and when they batted. After all, we had four Test match bowlers in our line-up (five if you include myself, which I'd say you couldn't!) Northumberland didn't win but they made it an excellent match and a great day out. Thanks, lads.

Victory gave Essex a second-round tie against Warwickshire at Edgbaston. Difficult but not impossible, we felt. So we had a good lively train ride back to London the next morning, thinking things were going along fairly well for us. It had been, one way and another, a good week for us. And we each had a glass or two of milk to celebrate!

9

Trust 'Both'!

Long before summer, the real thing, had finally broken over
England to give blue skies and hot days – and allow Jane and I to
switch off our central heating at home! – the name of one man had
dominated the headlines of the English press. Ian Botham, my old
mate, seemed to be in trouble right up to his neck. There were
stories still rumbling on, like thunder, from goings on during the
West Indies tour; then disciplinary commissions at Lord's. All that
was followed by more showdowns with senior officials, banner
headlines, big stories. Trust Both – I just hope he has shares in all
these papers he helps fill. If so, he must be worth a fortune. The
drinks will be on him when I see him next time!

The upshot of the first commotion was that Ian found himself
banned from all senior first-class cricket until the end of July.
English cricket fans were saddened by that; Somerset were saddened and had to plan their revival in the County game without
the services of their brilliant all-rounder – and I was sad for Both.
I've an idea what being thrown out of cricket meant to him. Ian
loves the game; his life revolves around it. Take it away from him,
and you deny him something he cherishes. England, too, felt the
void. They had to take on the Indians without one of the best all-
rounders the game has ever seen. His loss was felt. That much was
plain to see.

I sat back and read the stories. I digested some of the more
serious ones, threw away others intent only on sensationalism. Ian
could do without that aspect at such a time. I could never remember
any one sports person creating as much newspaper space as Ian

Botham. I reckon most of the English tabloid papers would close down in a few weeks if Both packed up the game and emigrated! I honestly wonder what they would write about.

Of course, this was nothing new. Much of the same had been going on throughout the winter, from what I could gather. Firstly, through Botham's famous walk from John O'Groats to Land's End, which he did with some friends including my own brother. And then, less happily, during the England tour of the West Indies. The stories which came out of that trip were incredible. Was it a coincidence that for the first time really, lots of non-sporting journalists made the trip? Did that factor have anything to do with so many non-cricketing stories being sent home?

Even by his own extraordinary standards, it had been an incredible nine months for Ian. A grand walk for charity which helped sick children; failure in the West Indies laced with the whiff of scandal; to be followed by a ban for two months once he got back home. And then, as an after-dinner bitter mint, another row over a speech he gave in Manchester.

I had been expecting the fuss to die down once Ian was out of the limelight for a while. After all, there isn't much scandal you can attach to a bloke going salmon fishing in Scotland, is there? But I was wrong. Soon, papers were screaming headlines like: 'Botham calls Test selectors gin-soaked dodderers' . . . Oh, no, not more!

Apparently, Both had been assured what he said at a private testimonial dinner in Lancashire, would remain between him and his audience. No press men were to be allowed in. So Both gave a light-hearted speech with a bit of spice. You couldn't really expect him to go up there and tell a load of men who had enjoyed a good few drinks and a lively evening, all about the merits of his mother's style of knitting, could you? But the inevitable happened. Some rat leaked the story. I heard a journalist talked his way in and tape-recorded the whole thing. And then sold it to Fleet Street. Sordid in the extreme, but Both was back in the soup. It began to seem like his second 'home'!

This time, despite as much speculation in the media, the authorities turned a blind eye. They probably took credit for that. After all, the speech should never have been made public, it wasn't intended to be. And it was at a private function. I guess anyone is entitled to their own private views on other people, whatever they may say. It wasn't as if Ian called up a national newspaper and said: 'I want to launch an attack on the Test selectors'.

I've known Ian Botham for a few years now and I'm pleased to say he is a friend of mine. I like the guy, I enjoy being in his company. But I do feel he is one of the least understood men ever to have played sport at the highest level and therefore been exposed to the public eye. There are two reasons for that – Ian Botham himself, and the people who purport to be genuine press writers. Some of them ought to be ashamed of the things they have written about Both over the years.

You have got to admit that Both is a rogue. A very likeable one, but a rogue all the same! He doesn't always do things which are considered as being on the straight and narrow. But then you can't have it all ways. England was quite happy to see Both go out and smash the 1981 Australians all over Yorkshire and Lancashire, in those two Test matches, to turn the series and win the Ashes. An ordinary guy couldn't have done that, only one with Botham's remarkable attitude to life and its problems. The man has a go, he's unconventional and he gets unconventional results on the cricket field. Look at that Headingley match – England still runs short of avoiding the follow-on with just three wickets left. And they end up winning the game. It was only through Botham's extraordinary brilliance. And I don't believe you can expect a bloke to play like that one minute and then go off the field, have a glass of milk to celebrate and go home to an early bed. Life doesn't work like that.

I just don't believe people have got the right impression about Both. Partly, as I say, because of Both himself but also because of what has been written about him. To my way of thinking, the guy is no Al Capone type. If he were, I'd say go ahead lads, dig up what you can on the fellow and keep him away from society. But this is the world of fantasy. Both is a tremendous cricketer and a really nice bloke to those who know him. He didn't have to walk the length of Great Britain to raise almost £1 million for a charity for children suffering from leukaemia. And he didn't have to fly all the way up to Yorkshire, as he did during his ban from cricket this summer, just to visit a sick child who the family felt might respond to hearing Both's voice at his bedside. Do out-and-out rotten guys do such things? Not to my knowledge. Yet the papers tear the guy apart. His character is assassinated. Maybe part of that is because other papers who don't get his exclusive column feel jealous. I don't know. But I feel there's more to it than that.

There seems to be something in the British character which

makes people want to see a guy get on to a pedestal but then try to knock him off it. That's not the way in the United States – their sporting heroes are heroes for life. Admittedly, in Australia, while you are up there if you give a couple of bad performances they try and drag you down a bit. But nothing like this country – this is the worst.

What's that joke they say about three guys who see a guy driving down the street in a Rolls-Royce. The first, an Australian, says: 'Gee, look at that guy, lucky blighter. Oh hell, let's go and have a few beers.' The second, an American, says: 'Wow, What a motor! I can't stay here drinking fellows – I want one of them. And I'm, off to do some work to get it.' And the third guy, an Englishman, says: 'Look at that blighter. Why should he have that car and I've only got an old banger. It's not fair. Not right.' Maybe there's a true word spoken in jest, as the saying goes.

No one is saying Ian Botham is squeaky clean. But then if we all examine ourselves and what we have done in our lives, who can say they are ... really? Maybe the trouble with Ian is that he doesn't help himself. I don't think he goes out of his way to have a good rapport with the press, for instance. He has been known to manhandle press guys and has been very hard to get at. He can be very difficult in questioning. And I guess the press have their method. If a bloke is quite easy to talk to and gets on with the press and tries to do the right thing, I think they in turn try to do the right thing by that person. But if they have had a bad time from a guy, they tend to jump on him when the chance arises. An eye for an eye sort of judgement! Therefore, Ian has caused animosity with the way he treats the press. And the thing about Both is that he doesn't do anything by halves. Everything is bigger and better with Both.

You won't catch me apologizing for saying I like being in Ian's company. I enjoy having a drink or a meal with him. And I don't feel he is about to get me into any sort of strife. So you take as you find, don't you? Ian has done what he's done in private but he certainly hasn't brought it out into the open as far as I'm concerned.

Perhaps Ian doesn't appreciate just how big he has become and therefore what an impression he makes with people. He is the best known sportsman in the country and yet he doesn't realize that what he does is so noticed. His whole life is under a microscope and he ought to be more aware of that. I know full well that if I'm going to have a barney with my missus, the front lawn isn't exactly the place to have it, because next day, the chances are it will be all over the papers! But that means coming to terms with the fact that people are watching your every move. It sounds crazy and it is. After all, you're only a sportsman doing what you do best. And people don't watch the every move of top financial experts, who can make millions more in money than even the best cricketer. It's one of life's unexplained mysteries, isn't it, why people want to follow sports people so closely.

Now 'Both' is a lot different to me in that respect. If a bloke starts to give me a hard time in a bar, I tend to walk away from it. For a start it's not in my character to get involved. And anyway, I'm too small. But 'Beefy' isn't the sort of bloke to stand down. He doesn't seem to realize that if you end up bopping some bloke who is being a nuisance, it's going to be no big deal. In that respect, I'd say Ian has been naïve.

I will say this about Ian – I feel sorry for him having to put up with all the constant publicity. It would drive me nuts, and I can see what it has done to Ian. He has changed a lot in character, from his early days when I first knew him. Then, he was a lot more flamboyant. He was prepared to go out, have a drink, have a good time after a game, be seen in public. Always there were jokes and laughs. Now he seems more serious. I don't believe he enjoys going out at all because everywhere he goes, he gets hounded.

We saw that on the Australian tour to England in 1985. Ian and his wife Kathy, myself and Jane all went out to Langan's restaurant in London. Now that's not a small bistro tucked away in a hard-to-find side street! And when we went in, a lot of the people I saw, I'd watched on various television programmes in the UK. So they weren't exactly unknowns. But when Ian Botham walked in, it was like the King arriving for dinner! Every head turned. All eyes were on him.

We had a meal and then got outside afterwards to be met by a blaze of flashlights! Someone had tipped off the press we were there and they turned up in force. They were probably hoping to catch us with a couple of birds. But sadly for them, we were with our wives, our pregnant wives! The joke was on them that time. But that's the kind of thing Ian is getting all the time. And I for one couldn't handle that. I don't mind being asked about my cricket life. But I wouldn't enjoy that constant harassment.

Ian was banned for two months from all senior cricket, for his revelations that he used drugs earlier in his life. Fact. And I'm not about to pass my own particular judgement on that. Fact.

Drugs? What I'll say is that for me, there are enough highs in life to live well without using artificial stimulants. Every time I see my wife and family I get a 'high', if you want to call it that. It's a great pleasure, something I always look forward to. Things like that offer the elation I seek in life. So I don't feel I need anything else.

Ian? He's done it all and he's only thirty. He's got a good bank balance, is incredibly well known, flies a helicopter, and has done just about everything possible in cricket. Maybe he has got bored with his lifestyle. But looking ahead and being positive, I'd like to think he will come out of it all, wiser. It just worries me a little that guys of particular brilliance, often in sport, have sometimes hit their own self-destruct button in the past. I hope and I pray Ian doesn't do that because he's too nice a guy.

If he wants to, Ian can go on playing at the top level for another five years. That's if he gets this out of his mind and concentrates on his cricket. Dennis Lillee retired at thirty-five, Richard Hadlee and Imran Khan, both in the mid-thirties, still play very success-fully. Bob Willis was past thirty-five when he packed up. It all comes down to your motivation and fitness. If you have both of those and your desire is still there, then there is no reason why you cannot play beyond that time. I've a feeling you'll see a guy like Hadlee play on for a while yet. And why not? Heck, he's still one of the world's greatest bowlers. New Zealand would certainly feel the draught if he retired. But whether Ian will get the spark needed to play for that period of time, I don't know. Frankly, I doubt it. I give him another one or two years and then I expect him to look for something else to do. Both always needs a fresh challenge, it's in his nature. Already, he has talked of doing this Hannibal trek up through the Alps and that would be far more interesting to him than playing cricket. Why? Because he's done plenty of the latter. And a guy with his flair and zest for life needs new adventures.

Me? Don't put me in the same category as Ian. He has done so much, achieved so much and created so much publicity. Other guys are not the same. Look at Viv Richards – he is still churning out the big innings for West Indies. And the captaincy of his country has, like I experienced, probably offered a new incentive. Cir-cumstances are quite different for Ian. But whatever happens, I hope he will remain a close friend of mine. I do honestly hope he can come out of all this and put it behind him. Perhaps, too, people will start to remember he is a great cricketer and let him get on with playing his cricket and having some privacy in his life.

To many people, myself included, his ban for two months in 1986 achieved nothing. It was a negative sort of outcome. If the authorities were really fair, they should either have banned him for longer or not at all. Maybe a suspended type sentence would have been better. Perhaps that could have been done along the lines of an official saying: 'This is what we expect of our cricketers, you know the rules. Break them again and you are out for life.' That sort of ultimatum would have been better. But a two-month ban seemed little more than an appeasement for all the trouble and dramas. It was linked to all the speculation in the press that — he would be banned for months; he would be banned for life; don't ban Ian Botham; all that sort of stuff. At one time, I thought they might find a modern-day equivalent of your infamous Judge Jeffreys, the guy who became known as the 'Hanging Judge' at the time of the Monmouth rebellion! Don the old black cap and pass sentence!

To think that I used to reckon I had problems! I was even threatening to resign the captaincy of Australia over much more minor matters! Thank God people weren't writing stories about me saying I stuck needles in my arm and snorted drugs just before I went out to bat. You couldn't play cricket under those circumstances. And on that note, finally I'd just like to add that I find such stories ludicrous. About Ian Botham or anyone else. I don't know whether people realize how much physical exertion it takes to do what Ian Botham does. Run in, day after day, bowling as many as twenty-five or thirty overs usually when it's hot, which tires you out. And then going out there with a bat and smashing fours and sixes around the ground. With the reflexes needed to do that, there is no way in the world you could be doped up on drugs. No way whatever. It is just a physical impossibility. You don't half get some silly stories around the circuit. That one probably beats the lot.

As for Ian, long term, I wish him well. And I'd like to go on record as saying: 'You're welcome in my house, whenever you're over in our part of the world, mate'.

10

England's season of woe

Some people might have painted Ian Botham as a cross between the Boston Strangler and the male half of Bonnie and Clyde. But I honestly wonder what they think of some sportsmen who really take off when it comes to crazy behaviour. I could hardly contemplate the story (a true one, as well, apparently) about the British rugby player who had a problem with doors on a tour a few years ago. He didn't believe in opening them so he walked straight through them. He was a big lad, too – that must have been an expensive little habit by the end of the tour! Now I'm not saying that Australian cricket teams go on tour and behave like choirboys. We're certainly not up at seven o'clock in the morning, on our prayer mats. But I do like to think we pick and choose our moments to let our hair down. We certainly don't go in for smashing up places, as a pastime!

After we had beaten England at Lord's in the Second Test in 1985, we all went out and had a thoroughly big night. And when an Aussie says that, he means it! Good food, washed down with lots of decent beer. Yes, that's right, we found a place which specialized in Australian beer! But although we knew we'd had a few drinks, we didn't come home and use the hotel furniture as weight-lifting equipment. Nor did we hurl it into the street outside. And I promise you there were no bonfires of wooden tables, either! Occasionally, there will be a bit of slight damage like a table getting broken. Or maybe a heavy guy will get pushed against a door and the hinge will go. But from what I've heard goes on at times in other sports, it's all pretty innocuous stuff. And even if anything is broken, the tour management takes a dim view of it. If you really got stuck in and smashed things up, I wouldn't be surprised if you got sent home. That would be about par for the course. There would be a heavy fine and worst of all, you'd probably never get picked to play for Australia again. And I'm all in favour of that tough line. It is sensible, hard but fair discipline. Every guy who goes on tour knows the rules. If any one bloke is stupid enough to step so far out of line, he has to accept the consequences, in my book.

I'm happy to say that I believe cricketers realize their responsibility to the general public and to future players. It's no good staying at the best hotels in London and smashing up the rooms. Because the next time a team comes over, they won't have them. So you have a responsibility to your country and fellow players to behave properly.

Maybe the fact that rugby is such a physical game means those guys need a release valve. I don't know. And in rugby, you might not be playing a match for two or three days or even longer, so you can have more big nights out. In cricket, if you've got to be up early the next morning, either to play in a game or travel, you can't afford to be out half the night partying. It soon shows. And with twenty or so other blokes around to notice the bags under the old eyes, you won't keep it a secret for very long!

Rugby Union players are also classed as amateurs. Cricket is professional; it is my living. I'm not about to do anything which will end that living. I'd be an idiot if I did. Cricketers the world over, it seems to me, take their sport very seriously. You only have to turn up at a Test ground a good two hours before the scheduled start of play. You'll see all the players either having a net or stretching, going through a series of exercises. We have done that with Essex this summer. You're on the ground by 9.30 at the very latest. And after all the work-outs, you play all day, finishing by about 6.30 or sometimes later. By the time you have changed and got home, you've been away at your work for around twelve hours. And that's a long day. Don't get me wrong; I'm not complaining. I count myself terribly fortunate to be getting paid for playing a sport I love. It's the ideal set up for me. But the point is, it is your life and career, the way you earn your money. So you have to treat it as such and take it seriously. A professional attitude is needed all the time.

One cricketing country which illustrated that in almost everything they did in 1986, was India. They beat England 2–0 in a three-match series; a magnificent result for them. And they deserved it, too. England could not match them in batting, bowling and fielding skills. Yet it puzzled me the way England struggled. For when I first arrived in England in April, I told Graham Gooch the side I thought England would have most trouble with this summer would be New Zealand. I was fairly well clued up on India and New Zealand because we played them both from December 1985 to March 1986. I suggested that if England could overcome Richard Hadlee in particular and Ewen Chatfield, plus get Martin Crowe and Jeremy Coney out, then they would have a good chance of knocking over the Kiwis. So much for the form book and my assessment! Suddenly, the Indians start playing brilliant cricket and win the series handsomely.

Of course, it is only conjecture to say what might have happened if Ian Botham had been playing against India. But you cannot ignore the fact that your sides were bowled out by the Indians. However, if Both had been coming in at No. 6, I think it would have added enormous strength to your line-up. Both can take apart most attacks in the world when he's in the mood and he must have made you stronger. But from the end of 1985 when England beat us, their whole world was blown apart. And I reckoned they were still suffering from the fall out when the Indians cleaned them out.

England suffered two major blows in losing Ian Botham and the sacking of David Gower as captain. That certainly can't have helped things in the dressing room. Suddenly Gower's right to be captain was in question; Ian Botham's right to be classed as a genuine world-class all-rounder was under fire because he didn't make many in the West Indies. And then Allan Lamb's future as a Test batsman was being examined ... all sorts of things came out of that tour. In addition, the guy who caused us so much trouble, Tim Robinson, returned to England from the Caribbean looking very shaky as holder of an opening place. And Goochie had lost some form.

So five of your first six batsmen were under the microscope for a variety of reasons. Was it any great surprise India took advantage of the situation to win the series? You just started off the season on the wrong note and stayed that way. The Indians had played reasonably well without being brilliant against us in Australia back in December and January. But if England's recent history had not been so uncertain it would have been different because it comes down to frame of mind. And I doubt whether your guys were in the right frame of mind when they went into those Tests.

I'd want to reserve judgement on the Indians. For example, a bowler like Maninder returned figures, at times, which were pretty incredible. Something like ten overs for 11 runs, sort of spell. Whether he is that good a bowler remains to be seen. Curiously, the Indian bowlers seemed to get more swing and seam from the conditions and their batting seemed to adapt better to difficult wickets like Headingley. Vengsarkar made two very good scores on that wicket and the others hung around to help him. In that way, the Indians dominated not one but two or three of the Tests. At Lord's, however, it would have been a draw but for a poor second innings batting performance by England. All through the two summer series, though, I had the feeling England were still suffering from the traumas of the West Indies. Like rum, it took a while to get out of their system perhaps!

The selection process during the summer involved deciding whether there were better replacements available for players like Allan Lamb who had lost a bit of form. Far be it from me to tell England who to pick in their sides. But all I'd say is that more often than not I favour the policy of sticking with an established player in the belief that his luck will turn. Typically, the day after Lamb was dropped, he made 150 against good opposition on a suspect track at Hastings. And Wayne Larkins, one of the guys they wanted to bring in, didn't get any at all to speak of.

Personally, I wouldn't have dropped Lamb. To me, he is class; proven quality. Statistics don't always tell the true story and besides, I rate Lamb very highly indeed. I know he hadn't made more than about 60 for England in a long while. But I reckon there was a reason for that, certainly against us in 1985. In that series, he was batting at No. 5 whereas he had scored three centuries against the West Indies from No. 4, the previous summer. Paying the price of tinkering with success? Well, perhaps that's right . . .

Against us, it was amazing how many times England were at a big score when Lamb got to the wicket. They were 186 for two, 358 for two, 148 for two, 463 for two and 375 for two. A guy still waiting to go in at scores like that had some wait. And then when Lamb did get in, it was usually make or break. He didn't have the opportunity to get in and play a long innings because England needed quick runs and a continuation of the momentum. Lambie may have suffered from that. Had he been at No. 4, he would have found himself in the position Gatting enjoyed – that is having the time to settle and build a big innings. And look at Gatting's form – two centuries and three half centuries, in that series. That could have been Lamb scoring that lot with Gatting waiting to come in at No. 5. Switching a position down the order doesn't sound like a lot of difference. And sometimes it isn't. But in that particular set of circumstances, it was.

You couldn't blame Lamb for failing to come to terms with it in the West Indies. No one did, except perhaps Gower. And he ended up getting the sack! As captain, anyway. As for Lamb, I still don't believe any England player brought in was a better player than Lambie.

When I look around the County circuit, I see only one player who is screaming out, through his form, to be in the England side. That player looks the best young player in England; he stands out head and shoulders above any other batsman. But his name is Graeme Hick of Worcestershire. He looks an exceptional player but England cannot play him for seven years because he is a Zimbabwean. Great news for us Australians, the Indians, the Kiwis and the rest! Not so good for you Poms. I bet you wish he could come into the Test side tomorrow because he looks good enough. It's a shame for him and for England he will have to wait so long. He's only twenty now and if he takes that talent into the Test match arena and it stands up to the examination there, Hick could create a magnificent name in seven years. Instead, he won't play Test cricket for that time. A pity – the world game needs young players of his flair and talent.

I know that Worcestershire are absolutely chuffed that they've got him and no wonder. Any county would be! To be able to produce that kind of scoring at twenty (he got 2,000 runs in 1986), suggests a rare talent. And it must be particularly frustrating for him that England are picking players like Chris Smith, Neal Radford and Allan Lamb, all of them born in Southern Africa, for their Test team. Yet he has to wait seven years.

I don't see any other player around with Hick's ability. When the lad fails, he seems to score half centuries! Some failure! Perhaps I can persuade him to seek Australian citizenship. He'd go down a bomb on the Hill at Sydney, if he was batting for Australia, I can tell you.

Robert Bailey of Northamptonshire looks a good player. But he may have to tighten up a little in his all round play, to adapt to

Test cricket. Cricket at international level is about pressure, tension and the general standard of bowling is very strong. You don't get too much rubbish thrown up at you. So your technique does come under scrutiny. If you have too many flaws you might be an initial success but then you will be sorted out. Bailey gets on with the game and he's not scared to hit the ball in the air. That's not a bad sign in a youngster. And we all start off our Test careers the same. There is always room for improvement when you're a young player coming on to the scene. But because of the demands of the game at that level, you either come to terms with it fairly quickly or you don't.

A couple of decisions the England selectors made had me puzzled. I began to think there was some grand conspiracy afoot to fool the Australian captain who might have been trying to pick up a few tips for the forthcoming Ashes series in Australia in late 1986. If so, I'd award first-class honours degrees to the selectors, for they had me baffled!

Wayne Larkins was chosen when he'd made, I think I read, 43 runs in six innings. I felt terribly sorry for Wilf Slack when I heard Larkins had replaced him. Slack went to the West Indies in an emergency, battled hard in the last Test over there and got runs and then got picked for the Second Test over here against India. But he missed out, scoring-wise, on a wicket which most batsmen found hard to score runs from. Then he was dropped for the next Test. It was quite beyond me.

Graham Dilley seemed a bit wayward against the Indians. But I put that down to the fact that he had got out of the habit of going all day. A quickie has to come back after his first spell, bowl another six or seven overs, have a rest, and then perhaps bowl two more spells in the day. Because of his long absence, Graham was still easing himself back into the Test match scene. But he has the quality to stay in there and succeed.

England must have felt Richard Ellison's form was very dis-appointing after the way he machine-gunned down our batsmen, the previous summer. He didn't seem to have the same penetration as before and didn't swing it as much. Perhaps he's like a good few English bowlers – let them see a guy at the other end holding a bat and wearing a baggy green cap, and he'll become a man inspired! That's what I suspect, anyway. I've got a good pal I've talked about already in this book who seems to specialize in that sort of thing. But I'm not mentioning his name again!

One thing which is strange about the England bowling selection, I have noticed before this summer. When England go for only one spinner in their side, they always seem to pick John Emburey and leave out Phil Edmonds. Or, at least, that has always seemed to be the case up till now. But when both are picked in the same side, Edmonds always seems to bowl the most overs. I don't understand the logic behind that. For me, it's a pleasure to watch them bowling in tandem because I regard the sight of two quality spinners at work, as one of the highlights of the game of cricket. It's a sight which is all too rare these days. And in the case of Edmonds and Emburey, they do seem to work well together.

You can afford to have two spinners in your Test side in England, if you have a couple of all-rounders. It seems to work quite well that way. But without someone like Ian Botham to march in at No. 6 and plunder the bowling, the tail starts to look a bit exposed.

England's tail seemed to become rather long in 1986. All the players tried from No. 6 down seemed to be about the same standard without being exceptional batsmen. All capable of getting a 40 or 50 for you but if you looked at averages, they probably wouldn't be averaging even 20. So you run into trouble, like you did against India, when you come up against a side which can winkle you out. If your early batting hasn't done especially well and you're relying on the tail to pick up another 100 runs you can find yourselves in difficulties. And that's exactly what happened against the Indians.

By contrast, their tail seemed to wag about as much as a dog with three bones! They looked as though they batted down to No. 11. I saw Roger Binney batted in most of the Tests down at No. 8 or 9. Yet that guy has opened the innings for India before now! Guys like that who go in low down are capable of playing the decisive role in a Test match. You get a team at 340 for seven and think they're almost out. But they end up making 450 and more often than not, it proves to be the difference between success and failure. And the frustration for the fielding side – it's awful. One of the worst experiences in the game.

11

'Seventy-one is, well, seventy-one!'

The uncertainties of County cricket in England are legendary; I reckon you could be more certain of trends on a merry-go-round like the Stock Market. If anyone needed further proof of that argument, eleven days early in July provided it in the experiences of Essex. Not to put too fine a point on it, we were blitzed three times in three crucial games. We suffered a major setback to our season.

July started with the touring New Zealanders at Chelmsford. It was a game I played in, although several of our top-line players missed the match through Test match calls or a rest. So with a young side, it wasn't a great surprise that we lost to the tourists. What we did see during that game was further proof of Martin Crowe's tremendous quality. For me, the guy is now the best young player in world cricket. I don't make that judgement casually, either – I've seen a lot of Martin in the past twelve months and I can't say I've seen anyone better. For his age, he is exceptional.

You have the incredible situation of Martin, still only in his mid-twenties, being the linchpin of the New Zealand batting. And not only that, he plays as though oblivious of the pressures. The guy looks a natural. He played a tremendous innings against us (100 not out). OK, our bowling was under strength. But that still didn't make it easy for him. You have to possess a rare talent to play like he did.

I guess some people might class him with Richie Richardson or

Greg Ritchie. But both have more senior players of whom things are expected in their Test sides. Martin doesn't. It is an incredible responsibility to have at his age yet he has come to terms with it very well.

Over the next eight or nine years, Martin Crowe should go on to dominate bowling attacks throughout the world. He plays the same sort of game against anyone and is as much at home against spin as fast bowling, Already, the big scores are coming, even in Tests; a sure sign of true quality. He got 188 against the West Indies in Guyana and then 106 against England at Lord's in the First Test in the summer of 1986. And he took 188 off Australia in the Brisbane Test in 1985.

On top of that little lot, he is a tremendous one-day cricketer. He can bowl handy medium pacers, is an excellent catcher of the ball and he's quick around the field. When he's batting, he hustles you with his speed between the wickets, turning ones into twos and twos into threes. He can improvise a shot to find the boundary in a limited-over game, or build an innings steadily, as he did against England at Lord's. It seems to me there really isn't very much the guy can't do.

Around forty-eight hours after we'd seen the young master, Martin Crowe, at work, we copped a lengthy sight of an old veteran, Clive Lloyd, at just about his best. I'm all for watching good batsmen at work, but this was becoming something less than a pleasure because both times we were on the receiving end of the stick. And it was about as pleasant as having a stubborn old molar tooth pulled out:

Essex had gone to Old Trafford for the weekend programme against Lancashire. It was obviously an important game in the hunt for the Championship. And what a shock we had in store. We lost the toss on the Saturday, the first day of the Championship game – and I knew we had problems, even before we went out to bat. It was an overcast, heavy day and there was quite a lot of grass and a bit of moisture in the wicket. Lancashire put us in as soon as they won the toss, which is precisely what we would have done to them, had we called correctly. Possibly with the same results!

Certainly, what happened to us was disastrous, to say the least. We were all out in thirty-two overs . . . for 71! Lancashire were at full strength, but we were five short because of the Test, and injuries. You don't like to make excuses, but five blokes is almost half a team. That counts.

Lancashire exploited the conditions fantastically well. But 71 is, well, 71. And you can't justify that really. Patrick Patterson was our chief executioner, with six for 46 in twelve overs. From what we heard afterwards, it was his first long spell of really quick bowling all summer, at a sustained pace. Thanks for saving it up for us, pal!

I've been in sides which have been bowled out for under 100 before now. But I couldn't remember one as low as 71. There is always a sense of disbelief when it happens because you always think some pair will get in and stay together. And then perhaps you'll scratch out 150. But 71 means a whole side has been knocked over. Patterson was too much for us all, but Don Topley surprised him near the end by hitting him away for a couple of boundaries in one over. Compared to what had gone before, it was like tasting sugar after cyanide! Don made 15 not out, our top score. I made only six, before falling to Paul Allott who finished with the extra-ordinary figures of 12 overs, 7 maidens, 10 runs, 2 wickets. The ball had moved around a lot and fizzed off a difficult pitch. But Lancashire still made 177 for five off 74 overs by the close.

To suffer that sort of humiliation is awful because it leaves you virtually without hope for the rest of the match, unless you knock the opposition over very quickly, too. We didn't do that – they made 240 – and our second innings wasn't a lot better. Twelve for two became 61 for three until Alan Lilley and myself got together to take the score to 124 for three. But when Alan went, we crumbled to 147 all out and defeat inside two days by an innings and 22 runs. Someone called it undignified – I could have found a stronger word, I think!

My 51 was of scant consolation. Hidden among that hiding, it was no sort of comfort whatever. Allott and Patterson both took four for 43. It was Lancashire's first Championship win over Essex for thirteen years. Yet at the start of the match, we were leaders of the Championship table and Lancashire were twelfth with only two wins from 10 matches. Which goes to show that you never know what might happen in an English County match.

Of course, it was our rank misfortune to be on the receiving end of Patrick Patterson's return to form. But credit to him – he bowled at real speed and looked to be improving all the time. Patterson is a very good illustration of English County cricket making West Indian Test sides strong. When I first played against him, he was playing down in Tasmania and wasn't particularly enjoying himself. He had a few personality clashes with the skipper and perhaps that affected his performance. But even then Patrick had all the ingredients of being a genuine pace bowler. It was just that he was a little wayward in length and line. Also, he didn't come back from his initial burst as well as someone with more experience. That is what marks out the best; a bloke like Malcolm Marshall who can bowl through a lengthy session at extreme pace and then return later at the speed he left off. That's the difference between a really good quality fast bowler and the blokes who can bowl quickly but can't seem to produce it at will. That was what Patrick used to be like.

The guy has clearly moved ahead from that stage. There was a marked improvement in Patrick's bowling when I saw him against us. Now, he doesn't only bowl quickly but he gets movement off the wicket and in the air. He has stamina and also bowls a good line and length. That all adds up to one unmistakeable fact – English County cricket has bred another West Indian fast bowling monster. And I don't mean that in a derogatory sense to Patrick! You have yourselves to blame for bringing on a guy who will now return to haunt you more and more at the highest level. And the rest of us, too, more is the pity! Whether he would have developed like this had he been playing only his own domestic cricket, we shall never know. But he's another who has proved the point – come to England and you learn the game.

By some margin, Patrick was the fastest bowler I had faced this year, together with Marshall and Daniel. There wouldn't be a lot of difference in sheer pace between the three but conditions at Old Trafford made Patrick seem a little bit quicker. '

You'll know, by now, that I seldom get out and walk into the pavilion calling for champagne to celebrate an innings! But I was particularly annoyed at my dismissal this time. In the first innings, I just nicked a good ball – a fair cop, as they say. But in the second, I played a very negative shot in the last over before tea. I was guilty of clock watching. I'm not blowing my own trumpet when I say it needed me to play a long innings if we were going to get out of jail. Why not? I was the most experienced guy in the batting line-up. Anyone was entitled to look to me for a big score. And I'd started to hit the ball quite well in that second innings. There weren't many dramas going on – for just about the first time in the match.

Cricket, however, is a devilishly unreliable game. Just when you think you've cracked it and it's plain sailing – whack. You get rocked back on your heels and everything looks completely different. In normal circumstances, I'd have been after young Watkinson a fair bit. He has only just started bowling spinners and I'd have wanted to stamp my authority. But in the last over before tea, I played safe – and paid the pènalty. Out, off bat and pad. I was very disappointed with myself.

It was like welcoming John Lever to the captaincy with a garland of thorns, too. John took over because Graham Gooch was playing in the Test, Keith Fletcher was injured and Brian Hardie was also missing, through injury. It was never really discussed whether I would take charge. And I was grateful for that. I had openly stated before I arrived, I didn't want that extra responsibility. I'd had enough of it with the Australians against New Zealand throughout last summer, as well as the Indians. So I wanted a rest. Anyway, I didn't think it would be fair on the County, myself or the other players because obviously there is a seniority there and they don't want me to come in and be picked as captain straightaway. As it turned out, John and myself got our heads together at certain times. But the final responsibility came down to him which was quite right because of his experience. Anyway, I don't think the Lever–Border twosome is going to run quite as long as your Morecambe and Wise duo. We didn't have quite the same success, did we!

Lancashire tried a different captain against us, Graeme 'Foxy' Fowler. And if the result was any indication, they ought to confirm him in the job as full time skipper. Because his side rolled us over without mercy! It's obvious Graeme has got real talent as a batsman. Anyone who has made 201 in a Test match in India, has proved that beyond all doubt. But he had an awful·spell in 1985 and then ran into another depressing patch in 1986 after a great start. Perhaps he proved better than anyone the way cricket can knock you down just as quickly as it builds you up. A few good scores and you're flying high! But then a run of bad scores follows, often for no apparent reason. And you're back down to earth with a real hard bump.

Graeme Fowler must be hard for anyone to analyse. Because he plays these long innings and then, a few days later, gets out for no real reason. People say he's iffy outside the off-stump but most left-handers have the same problem in that area. With right-hand bowlers bowling across us, we tend to get out caught behind the wicket a fair amount. It's a constant battle against that. I know – I've been at that stage.

One argument would say Graeme is too adventurous, too loose outside off stump. But another camp might claim left-handers always score a lot of runs through the offside, by driving or cutting. Which is right? Hard to tell. Certainly, if you tighten up too much in that area you might lose your ability to score runs heavily. And that's always been a trait of Graeme's play. He's a very exciting bat to watch when he's going well, too.

Having Clive Lloyd there as a mentor ought to have helped Graeme in the sticky times. Clive, of course, is also a left-hander and you do need to speak to a guy who plays the same style, if you feel things are going wrong.

Lloydie is the doyen of Lancashire cricket, and it's no wonder. He gets a huge reception whenever he goes out to bat. It's obvious he is so well loved and respected up there. Clive has given so much joy to so many people in that county over the years that his right to a place in that side is unquestioned. And even if you did challenge it, he'd have stuffed the argument back down your throat with the 91 not out he made for them in the Sunday League match that weekend. It was vintage Lloyd; even Paul Prichard's century afterwards couldn't win us the game because of Lloyd's effort.

I heard that Mike Brearley was critical of Clive's captaincy. Frankly, I suspect the two of them never really got on that well. At times, I do agree that anyone could be captain of a side with four fast bowlers as good as those Clive had had at his disposal in recent years. But as I've already said, there is and has been a lot more to Lloyd's captaincy of the West Indies. Overcoming all the inter-island rivalries is one of his greatest achievements. He welded them into a great team unit which, under another personality, might not have occured. And these days, West Indian sides are so professional, another testimony to Lloyd's influence.

Rivalries, which have developed from strong area backgrounds, can conflict once you get into a national side. In such circumstances you need a forceful leader. And that's where Clive has made his mark. He has given the West Indies the belief that they can win; he has instilled professionalism. Before him, they were entertaining, but win, lose or draw – that wasn't quite as meaningful to them. But Lloyd bred an attitude which made winning vitally important. They were just calypso kings before; now they're supreme competitors, as hard as nails to beat. So I wouldn't go along with

Mike Brearley's evaluation of the Big Cat's captaincy. I've got the utmost respect for what Clive has done for his country. Getting all that talent harnessed in one direction rather than going off in all different directions couldn't have been easy.

Now the Lancashire side Lloyd has helped develop looks as though it has promise. Certainly, it's very talented. I wouldn't be surprised to see them among the trophies in the next few seasons. Gehan Mendis is now producing the runs which he has the ability to score; Neil Fairbrother looks a very good cricketer to me, and with christian names like Neil Harvey, he can't go far wrong, can he?

An advantage Lancashire and Yorkshire enjoy is that they both have a very strong League system. They're both very competitive leagues. So all the young English guys are brought up in an atmosphere in which there are a lot of overseas stars playing. Therefore, they get used to seeing quality players at work and it ought to mean a very high standard. That has to stand them in good stead for when they crack it and reach the County scene.

No youngster could have witnessed a finer exhibition of batting than Clive Lloyd in action on Sunday, 6 July. It was exceptional. Lancashire were scoring at eight, nine and ten runs an over at will mainly because Lloyd kept hitting us out of the park. He found the gaps, especially early on when he took it nice and easy. Then came the acceleration with strokes of violent power. I had to rate it as just about the perfect one-day innings. We ended up two runs short that day but cricket won. It was an excellent game, although I'd have felt happier about it all if we'd ended up winners.

At the end of August, 1986, Clive Lloyd was forty-two. And although he might now struggle a bit against extreme pace, anything slightly off target or below that express pace gets the same treatment as it always did. He's probably playing as well now as he ever did. Certainly in my time playing against him over the last four or five years, he has played some magnificent innings. And it's amazing how many times he has got West Indies out of a jam. He seems to have produced his best knocks when they were struggling. Clive's example shows that age isn't any real barrier. As long as the old pins will get you out into the middle, you can still do it, even well past forty!

Can I see myself going on that long? Not likely. I'll be sitting back with the old carpet slippers on by then! But seriously, you can never tell. I'll bet at thirty-five Clive felt it was near the time to call it a day. And yet six years later he was still going strong.

Perhaps that second wind comes along and encourages you. I'll see when I'm at that stage.

Some days you feel like you could go on until you're fifty. On others, you want to pack up that night. Just twenty-four hours after our Championship defeat by an innings against Lancashire, we were on our way down the M1 from Birmingham, our title of Natwest holders a thing of the past. What a week!

Losing our title was really the final nail in the coffin for us. Everyone including ourselves expected us to beat Warwickshire. No disrespect to them, but we thought we ought to be capable of a victory. And when you're the holders, well, more is expected of you, rightly so. But it turned out to be one of those performances – bad from the word go. Like the actor who goes on stage and fluffs his opening line. Then things get worse from then on.

We didn't bowl well with the new ball and Warwickshire got away to a roaring start. They put on 69 for the first wicket and that was a good base. Also, every time they hit the ball firmly it seemed to find a gap. When you see those little things happening, you think to yourself: Here we go, it's going to be one of those days.

John Lever bowled eleven overs for 63 runs, no maidens, no wickets, which was very unusual for him. Neil Foster did well to finish with three for 31 off 12 overs and really, Warwickshire's 255 from 59.5 overs didn't look an enormous score. We didn't feel as though we had to climb Everest to succeed!

Geoff Humpage made 70. He's one of those guys who chances his arm a bit. But he hits the ball murderously hard. And when it comes off, he scores well. Brian McMillan only made ten but he looks a good cricketer. He's a South African from Transvaal, but they say he struggles to get into the Transvaal top team. If so, they must have some side. This guy looks a very handy cricketer. His batting is probably a little bit better than his bowling at the moment. But as an all-rounder, he adds up to a very useful player.

All Warwickshire's players chipped in for that 255. And yet we thought we would get 256 to win. Although the ball was starting to keep a bit low and wasn't really coming on to the bat, you wouldn't have risked much of a bet against us when we reached 98 without loss, with Goochie still there. Young John Stephenson was with him. But they had taken a fair while to get those runs and when they were out, we lost seven wickets for 46 runs in just 16 overs. The wicket didn't explain that sort of collapse.

Gooch and Stephenson had set it up. Trouble was, the rest of the batting couldn't finish the job. Only Derek Pringle, with 33, hung around at all. I got just six before McMillan bowled me. It was an error of judgement on my part – the ball bounced on me a little bit and I chopped it on to my stumps. I seem to have been out that way a lot of times this summer. Basically, I put it down to the fact that I have been trying to play a shot I wouldn't normally attempt, back home. But in limited-overs cricket, the need is there to get on with it and you sometimes play shots which are pretty difficult. And they don't always come off. You're trying to run that particular shot down to third man area for a single or a couple. But the ball seems to have kept low on me a bit sometimes or bounced a bit more than I expected. The margin for error is slim with those shots. Perhaps I've got into some bad habits.

Our decline, from 111 for one to 191 all out, was desperately disappointing. The jokes weren't exactly flying around the dressing room at that stage. We only lasted 51.4 overs, too – a sorry end to Essex's Natwest title reign.

Graham Gooch battled it out for 48 that day. But even Goochie would be the first to admit it wasn't quite a virtuoso performance. This season, he has played the odd innings where he's gone out and flayed attacks alive in his usual, inimitable style. But only rarely. It hasn't been the Goochie everyone expects and that's probably because he has been through one of those periods where you just don't succeed.

You're not getting your feet in the right place. And, unlike when you're in good nick you meet the ball with the full face of the bat, in lean spells you tend to come through with the bat at a slight angle. Inches count at this level, too. It might not look much to the bystander. But if you close the face on the ball just a fraction you don't hit it where you intend to. And you certainly don't strike it as well. I worked out that as my problem earlier in the season. And I think Graham has been doing the same thing. You look for the ball and then push out at it but close the face a little. Whereas when you're flowing, you wait for the ball to come on to you and play it with the full face of the bat. That way, you get a little more time to play the shot. And your timing is there, too.

Certainly, the real Graham Gooch wasn't on view in the 1986 season. But perhaps that wasn't too bad a thing. People will enjoy him at his best all the more when he hits peak form again. There's nothing like the loss of something to make you want to see it again.

Why is it that because I come from Down Under, everyone wants
pictures of me with things upside-down?

Guess what has stopped play? Keith Fletcher doesn't look very concerned – he must be used to it.

Brrrrr ... eight degrees and probably dropping. It ain't half cold, Mum!

Essex's 1986 Championship-winning squad.

Power in the drive: go through the ball with precision yet aggression
(v. Gloucestershire at Chelmsford, Benson & Hedges Cup).

Maybe Dene, my little boy, fancies himself more as a footballer than a cricket player. West Ham, here he comes...

Perhaps I had been down on bended knee praying for better weather early in the season!

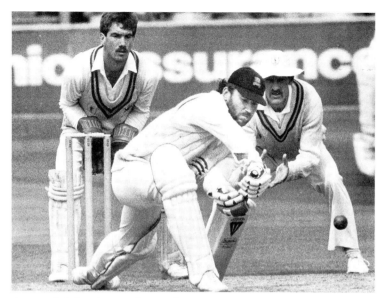

The forward defensive stroke, as demonstrated against Nottinghamshire in the Benson & Hedges quarter-final tie at Chelmsford.

Note Clive Rice's excellent poise at first slip: comfortable position, fingers outstretched, eyes on the ball.

A rare moment of aggression for me in the same match. I didn't last long, to my chagrin.

More trouble with the locals thinking everything is upside-down in Australia! The car saw good service on the County circuit.

We're into mid-summer – we must be. I'm on the front foot getting the ball away and looking for runs.

'What on earth is Ray East up to now, mate?' Essex's guru, the admirable Fletcher, looks suitably amused.

A face in the crowd at Northampton. I think (hope) I'm going out to bat, not coming in.

On the attack.

With Allan Lamb during the County Championship match against Northampton-shire. In my view, England paid dearly for their decision to drop Lamb during the summer. For me, the man is class, proven quality.

Packed and ready for the journey, but the slightly wistful look is understandable – I didn't want to go with a month of the season still remaining.

That's human nature, isn't it? When Graham Gooch is going full belt, there cannot be many better sights in the world game. He stands there and whacks you. Look out if you're a guy bowling just slightly off the mark. He'll smack you all around the place. Bowlers' extermination incorporated, that's Goochie at his best! Don't I know it. I've seen it at close hand enough times!

The name of Phillip Anthony Jason De Freitas might not have been instantly recognized around the County circuit at the start of the 1986 County Championship season. But by the end of it, the young Leicestershire all-rounder, who had been born in Dominica and educated in North London, had carved out a real name for himself.

On a day of unbroken sunshine at Southend, De Freitas announced himself to Essex in a very positive manner. And we certainly couldn't really blame the wicket. OK, it had a ridge in it at one end. But when we reached 115 for two after winning the toss, we seemed well on target for a good start to the first match of the Southend Festival week.

Brian Hardie had gone early, but Paul Prichard and myself got stuck in. Paul had passed 50, I was approaching the same stage. But De Freitas, who had come on as first change bowler, had a few shocks in store for us. He is only twenty, but he has tremendous potential. He proved to be one of those bowlers who is much nippier than they appear to be at first sight. He ambled in and let the ball go, but it was on you much quicker and earlier than you anticipated, De Freitas would probably be about the same pace as Neil Foster. But whereas with Foster you can tell from his action he is going to be nippy, De Freitas didn't look that quick . . . Until the ball arrived.

The problem was, the guy exploited the ridge marvellously well. His accuracy was terrific for a young bowler. With his pace and length landing the ball right on the ridge at one end, the ball would bounce six inches to a foot and then climb. You had a hard job to score runs off that stuff.

The wicket tended to become more bouncy after a fairly quiet start. So we tumbled, from 115 for two to 153 all out. De Freitas bowled me for 45, Prichard made 56 – and no one else got into double figures! It was the old pack of cards job, all falling down after the first one had been nudged.

OK, we felt; what's good for this guy, is going to be useful for us. But John Lever didn't bowl from the end which De Freitas had used, which we agreed afterwards was a mistake. If he had with his pace, he could have been just as dangerous. Don Topley used that end, but although he bowled well, he lacked the pace when it did leap a bit, to cause real problems.

'Daffy' De Freitas had finished with six for 42 off 17.5 overs, by far the best figures of his career. And he deserved them because he bowled a long spell and maintained his line and length. He knew he had to let the ridge do the job.

Leicestershire, however, were not exactly coasting by the end of the day. They were 154 for six with all the top batsmen gone. Or so we thought! But next morning, Clift got 46, Benjamin 25, De Freitas 19 (he showed he could bat a bit as well), Agnew 35 not out and Gill 17. They ended up 264 all out, a lead of 111. They batted well but had bagged all the luck that was going. The snicks flew over the top of the slips, the aerial shots into the outfield missed the fielders. At times like that, you feel like saying: 'Hey, where's our luck then? It's about time the pendulum swung back!'

With a lead of that size, we had problems. Or a problem. His name was De Freitas. We hardly made an ideal start – nought for one. And then 9 for three. Then 25 for five became 48 for six. We'd had it. But David East and Don Topley stuck around and we reached 111. Leicestershire needed one run to win.

De Freitas had skinned us. He bowled 16.1 overs, including 5 maidens, and took seven for 44. That gave him match figures of thirteen for 86! He got six of the first eight batsmen to fall, too. It was our second two-day defeat in succession and a rotten ending to the match. We had been absolutely outplayed. We were lucky to get as many as 111 in the second innings.

Jon Agnew bowled quite well in the game but didn't look as sharp as De Freitas. So that tells you something of the twenty-year-old's capabilities. He also did it into the breeze which was another plus point. The top bowlers didn't fancy battling into the wind so they missed using the ridge!

Leicestershire had been captained by Peter Willey because David Gower was away at the one-day international. Peter is a really hard man, a fighter who plays pace bowling very well indeed. But I've got to admit I was surprised when the England selectors brought him into the Test side for the first game of the series against the New Zealanders. Not surprised to see Peter, once in there, getting runs. He's a terrific competitor, one of the hardest around. But at thirty-six, he wasn't exactly a spring chicken. And if that was the English selectors' idea of a youth policy, with plans looking to the future, then I'd say it was a bit of a joke! I would have thought Peter's international career was over, not least because he's got a very bad knee. I felt there had to be someone else around the County scene who would be younger and could have been tried with an eye to the future. No disrespect to Peter – he remains a fine player. But I'll bet he was about as surprised as I was when I heard he'd been called up.

Our two-day defeat had left the sponsors with a problem. Lunches were booked for clients; there was no cricket scheduled. And after that heavy defeat I've got to be honest and say I didn't want to play in a Mickey Mouse, specially-arranged one-day game on the Friday. Competition is all to me – it is my motivation, my interest. A one-day game outside any competition, is not my cup of tea. These games just don't serve any great purpose, apart from providing cricket for the sponsors and officials. There is normally a special prize at stake, say £1,000 for the winners. And the money goes into the team fund.

I found the game that Friday hard work. I could understand the need for it because cricket might not survive without its sponsors; they play an increasingly important role. But I wanted to sit down and ponder my form and what had gone wrong for us in our last two matches. I didn't think I'd find many answers in a limited-over game of no meaning whatsoever. But as it turned out, we seemed to have been stung into action by what happened against Leicestershire. And Worcestershire, our Saturday opponents in the Championship at Southend, copped it fair and square.

Defeat had pushed us down to third place in the table, damaging our title hopes. Worcestershire were fifth. So we knew we had to play well to get a much needed win. I was looking forward to the game. I wanted to have a good, close up look at the young batsman who had been slaughtering attacks all over the country for much of the summer, Graeme Hick. But before he could show his value, Graham Gooch was also looking forward to the game. He'd made a brilliant 91 for England in the one-day match against New Zealand the previous day. And now at Southend, he unleashed, probably for the first time in the summer, the complete range of all his brilliant shots. The pace and bounce was more predictable than in the first match of the week, and Gooch took full advantage.

He stood there and smacked the ball all over the place. It was a really good knock.

At 214 for no wicket, we had what you might call, a decent start. John Stephenson then got out for 85, but Gooch went on to 151. I made 56 and Brian Hardie 34 not out as we reached 370 for five. And then before the close we took two Worcestershire wickets for 11, before Hick strode out to make 19 and put the score at 40 for two by stumps.

Perhaps it's unfair to judge on such a day. But Neal Radford bowled 23 overs and took two for 113. It wasn't only that evidence, however, which convinces me that he will always struggle at Test match level, for one big reason – he is a little short at 5 ft 11 in, for a fast bowler. It might not sound too bad. But I think bowlers of that stature always tend to struggle in Test cricket if they are picked as a strike bowler. You're not too worried about the bounce from a guy like that because it's not going to be too high. OK, Neal has got a lot of wickets in County cricket and he's a good bowler, don't get me wrong. But on superb batting pitches which you often find in Tests, he has to work harder for his wickets. And without that extra height to get greater bounce and perhaps induce surprise in a batsman, he would struggle.

Of course, the argument against that is that Malcolm Marshall is exactly the same height as Radford. True. But look at his explosive pace. That makes him entirely different. If Radford could bat at No. 6 or 7 as well as being the bowler he is, he'd be a very handy cricketer. But even so, he's not the worst around, is he? And his record in County cricket proves that.

Graeme Hick is a player I do believe will make a major impact in Test cricket – when he eventually plays at that level. He impressed me greatly at Southend. You can always tell a bit of class. He had time to play, wasn't fussy but started to play shots straight away. For a twenty-year-old kid, he is a fantastic player. He looks run-hungry to me, and I believe he'll make a stack of runs at County level, each year.

In the Sunday game, we made a very good score, 273 for six off 40 overs, with Gooch getting 94. But at 186 for two and Hick going well on 47, Worcestershire were going along at a good pace. But when Hick fell and a few others went, the rate climbed and it was too much for them. But one shot Hick played off Gooch impressed me enormously. OK, most guys can hit a six if they charge down the wicket and strike the ball just right. But Hick played a sort of front foot drive which he lofted, off Gooch, and it sailed out of the park. You've got to have immense power and timing to do that; there was no ugly thrashing of the ball. He's not afraid to lift the ball which I like. It's more exciting to watch if a guy is prepared to loft the ball, and the game needs some players like that.

Talk to so many old timers and they'll tell you the same thing. 'Keep the ball on the ground, son, and you lessen your chances of getting out.' Probably true. But I still maintain it's more exciting if you attack and go for the ball, even to the extent of lifting it occasionally. So, for me, Hick is sensational. I believe he'll be the new Graeme Pollock of world cricket. Tall, powerful, elegant, thrilling. And if he came to Australia, he would be qualified for Test cricket in four years, not seven which is the time over here. So if he fancies coming out to our country and qualifying, I'd be the first at the airport to greet him. I'd also try and rush things through for him so that he was available even sooner. Guys with that ability ought to be gracing the Test match stage. Now!

Worcestershire reached 98 for five on Monday morning. An excellent start for us on our worst day of the week. But Dipak Patel came in to remind everyone that talk in previous years about him possessing the ability to play for England, wasn't so wide of the mark.

Patel shouldn't have been there at all – he had a heavy cold and was advised not to bat. I wish he'd followed that advice! He finished with 128 and his side got 323, only 47 short of us. It's amazing how often you read stories about guys who have got bad fingers or pulled muscles or they're batting with a runner, yet they tend to pull off these good innings. I know myself that when you're in that situation, you tend to be able to concentrate a lot better. Don't ask me why, but it's so. You play a lot better within your own limitations. You're there just to survive, hoping they score at the other end. But you end up getting a good score yourself. Chris 'Kippy' Smith did it for Hampshire a few weeks later, when he had a damaged finger.

We helped Patel on his way by dropping him. And he wasn't the only one who escaped in that way. But the Southend wicket started to play a few more tricks on the third day. And apart from Graham Gooch who got 79 in our second innings (what a weekend he had), no one really came to terms with it on the last day. Worcestershire bowled us out for 202 but needed 250 to win. They never looked like doing so, once they had slumped from 53 for one to 98 for seven. They ended up on 158, we won by 91 runs and got the maximum 24 points to go back into second place in the Championship. Foster (five for 64) and Lever (four for 55) took all but one of the second innings wickets.

It was a good game of cricket; an excellent contest all the way through. No 'gimmies', no contrived result. Near the end, Steven Rhodes came in and made 33 not out. He was peppered a bit with the ball starting to leap a bit but he played the survival role very well. This set me thinking about wicketkeepers for England at the moment. And I'd venture the opinion that in England's case, it might be better to go for a somewhat lesser wicketkeeper but a slightly better batsman. Now I know that might sound contradictory in the light of what I said about Knott and Marsh. But both made runs for their countries. And Bruce French's bad luck is that although he's not a prolific run getter, it looks worse because he has come in at a time when numbers 7 to 11 in the England side are not reliable scorers. So if the early order doesn't make the runs, the tail is under pressure to do well. But a couple of times, they have been found out.

It's different if you've got a Botham coming in at No. 6 and perhaps Pringle at 7. You can then afford the best 'keeper even if he's not likely to make many runs. But without that strength down to No. 7, it's nowhere near as good a situation if the tail is suspect. That tail England played a few times this summer looked about level in ability. Probably they were all No. 9s. But some played at No. 7, another at No. 11. And without the thirties and fifties which tail-enders can score at Test match level, it puts a whole lot more pressure on your top batsmen. Wagging tails are one of the best psychological things to lift a side, and depress their opponents.

There ought to be room for both Botham and Pringle in the England side. Pringle hasn't done badly for England lately and has made important runs at times. He's also a steady bowler. What's more, despite what some people say, I still think Botham is capable of fulfilling a strike bowler's place. OK, Both's bowling isn't as good as it once was. He'd admit that, I suspect. He's not swinging the ball like he used to, but he's still a worthy foe. You don't take too many liberties with him, not if you want to survive. And his batting is better than it was. So where one aspect of his game has fallen off the other has improved. Anyway, the guy's got 350-odd Test wickets and 4,000 runs. End of argument, yes?

12

Driving down the Mall, along the Sussex Downs

We headed for London – and drove down the Mall to waving crowds! It felt quite nice to be in that position, especially for an Australian. Buckingham Palace lay ahead of us, thousands of people were lining the sides of the road as we passed. I could almost imagine being king of England for a day! But no, the people hadn't turned out to welcome Essex's cricket team to the capital for our County Championship game with Surrey at The Oval, starting the next day. They were there for a slightly different reason – the wedding of His Royal Highness Prince Andrew to Miss Sarah Ferguson. It was the same day as our first day at The Oval.

Among the crowds already gathered for the wedding and prepared to sleep out overnight to ensure a good vantage point, were some Essex folk. So when we drove past, on our way to the hotel we used in Kensington, we got some cheers! A few of the lads were doing the royal wave, or their imitation of it, anyway! It was all great fun. And it got us into the feeling of what the big day was all about. For me, the royal family is terrific. They are so well thought of in Britain. I get disappointed when people think they are wasting the taxpayers' money and that they don't do anything particularly good for the country. Rubbish, I say! They're the best advertisement you have got for your country. They generate so much good will between other nations and within the nation itself. You only have to see the response to a royal wedding or a jubilee to have that fact proven.

It looked as though there were some lively parties going on in and around the Mall that evening. People were mixing, communicating. That's not a bad testimony to what the Royal Family is capable of, is it? Bringing people together. It certainly doesn't seem to happen for anything else, does it? People might queue up for Wimbledon and the FA Cup final and that sort of thing, but there is nothing quite like a royal occasion. I was very impressed and I think the royal family does a very good job in PR, promoting this country. There is a standard there, a bit of solidarity. This royal link goes back through the ages and I believe they are a marvellous asset for Britain.

I watched the royal wedding, on and off the next day, before and after I had batted. I made 52 so I wasn't out there all day, and we totalled 243 for nine off 92 overs. The cricket wasn't so colourful or entertaining as the wedding just up the road. From what I saw, the wedding was very impressive. You wouldn't think you would sit there and watch for hour after hour, but you found yourself doing so.

The next morning, we reached 250 all out, to secure our third bonus batting point. But it hadn't been a great display. It was a very good wicket at The Oval and I felt we had got about a hundred less than we should have done.

Tony Gray took four for 50 off 28 overs and bowled very well. He is the new West Indies hope and is built in the mould of Joel Garner. Big and tall (6ft 7in) he is the sort of bowler who gets extra bounce because of his height. And it ends up being easier to head the ball, soccer style, than get a bat to it! Gray is just another in the long line of West Indian hopefuls who will be made into a very good Test match bowler by the English system. There was a little bit more in the track for the bowlers on that first day and Gray got all the help he could from the conditions. No way was it a difficult wicket to bat on, the reverse in fact. But Gray's height and bounce made him their best bowler.

Graham Monkhouse impressed me, too. He's on the spot, picks up a couple of wickets almost every time he bowls and he looks the good County professional. Some days he might chip in for five or six wickets but overall he has excellent control and just keeps it there or thereabouts. You're never that worried about his pace but he does nip the ball around the seam a little bit. I rated him the next best bowler to Gray, and Surrey will miss him I'm sure now that he has had to retire through injury.

David Thomas was a lively left-armer and rushed in. But perhaps there was a bit too much rushing. In bowling a couple of good balls, he gives you a few to hit. Without being disrespectful, I feel Thomas would get some stick in Australia on our wickets. He is bustling and is trying to get you out, and he bowls a few bouncers. But perhaps he gives you too many to hit.

Surrey didn't make the best of starts to their innings. At 16 for two we were entitled to consider our opening thrust pretty effective. But if I had thought we had finished a hundred short of what we ought to have made on that wicket, I reckoned we were about two hundred short by the end of the day.

Trevor Jesty strolled in at 16 for two and walked out hours later with 221 to his name. It was one of the most extraordinary turn arounds I've ever seen. From the word go, he hit the ball right in the middle of the bat, found the gaps and there was basically nothing we could do. We tried everything – bumping him with two back for the bouncer, spread out fields, all that sort of thing. It was like trying to get out of the way of a speeding car which kept coming right for you! Jesty plundered our attack. Certainly, Foster and Pringle would have strengthened our challenge. John Lever and Don Topley bowled well but the back-up wasn't as experienced or good as it might have been. That isn't to take anything away from Jesty – he was magnificent.

Alec Stewart made 67 and Monte Lynch 85. Both looked impressive, Stewart particularly so. He had time to play his shots, always a good sign, and he was prepared to hit the ball.

Jesty went on and on. And once Surrey had passed 350 for the loss of only three wickets, I became convinced he was making a mistake batting on. His strategy wasn't hard to work out. He thought he'd get Surrey as far in front as possible and then get us in for a quick twenty minutes or half hour that night. That way, he would have all the next day plus a bit the night before to bowl us out. But I wasn't convinced it would succeed.

Admittedly, when Surrey finally declared at 448 for five (in 95 overs, mark you!) they had a lead of 198. But I always felt they would struggle to bowl us out a second time on that wicket. It was by now a superb track. Had Jesty declared a hundred in front, he might have bowled us out and then had only about 150 to chase in the fourth innings. But he went on and on, even through periods when they weren't really smacking the ball around that much. I found it a bit strange. He obviously felt he was doing the right thing, but I had my doubts.

I went in next day at 41 for two, still 157 behind. Brian Hardie and myself put on 101 for the fourth wicket, in 27 overs. Gray was still a threat, bowling 24 overs and taking three for 73. But I went on to my third Championship century of the summer, finishing on 138.

Now you'd know by now that I'm seldom happy when I get out, but this time, I was furious. I played a shocking stroke against Surrey's spinner, Medlycott. It was a ghastly sort of heave across it which I missed. OK, I'd got 138 but at that stage the match had not quite been put out of Surrey's grasp. So I was doubly annoyed.

Luckily, Stuart Turner saw us through to safety with a gutsy 25 not out. But my dismissal at a crucial time shows you that you can never afford to relax in this game, even when you've got 138 to your name. We could still have lost the match and I knew it. If we had, I'd have blamed myself for throwing away the good work we had all done to force a draw.

We finished on 276 for seven, just 78 ahead. It was a long final day and disappointing for us in that we had nothing but safety and a draw to salvage from the match. That's always hard to do if you are without hope of victory. But we wanted to battle and show we could bat all day. Perhaps Trevor Jesty may have realized afterwards he did bat on too long. I don't know. It's always a difficult decision to make in those circumstances.

Our draw at The Oval earned us only five points, a disappointment considering the fact that this used up one of our games in hand on Gloucestershire, the County Championship leaders. We still had one more – they had played fifteen against our fourteen – but the gap now was 21 points. It meant nothing less than a win would be good enough to catch them at the top. But unfortunately the fixtures were not going to help us close that gap. The next day we began a seven-day break from all cricket while Gloucestershire went to Worcester for a Championship match. It meant they might draw even further ahead and at this stage, I think anyone would tell you it is better to have the points in the bag rather than a lot of games in hand. The uncertainties of the weather mean that you can never be sure of getting a result to a match. And if you stand 50 points or some such total behind another side, having two games in hand (and therefore a possible 48 points) might not mean very much if the weather turned.

Still, our week off could not be spent worrying about whether Gloucestershire might slip further away from us at the top. And besides, as well as the Championship, there was always the John Player League title, the race for which was just beginning to gather momentum. That Sunday we did not have a game but we stood only two points adrift of Hampshire, Northamptonshire and Nottinghamshire, all of them on 28 points. But Hampshire's massive 276 for three against Leicestershire at Southampton meant they would finish the Sunday programme top of the table. This time, Paul Terry did the bulk of the scoring, making 142. The Hampshire side proved time and again during the summer that they possess some of the finest strokemakers in England. Greenidge, Terry, the two Smiths, Nicholas, Marshall ... all super strikers of the ball when they get going.

I spent the weekend in unlikely surroundings for a first-class cricketer – the Isle of Wight. Ryde played an Old England XI and an old pal of mine from my days at Gloucestershire asked me if I would go over to play. So Jane and I left the children at home, with Jane's sister, and off we went, via the hovercraft, to the island. I thoroughly enjoyed it. The cricket was fun and we were almost killed with kindness. It was tremendous. We played that Sunday and had a bit of a look around the island the next day which was pleasant. A change is as good as a rest, so they say and I certainly enjoyed getting away with Jane, even if it was only for a couple of days. I'm always happy when I can take Jane with me. She tolerates an awful lot – I think most cricketers' wives do – so it's good to be able to do something together for a change.

The first-class programme might have come to a temporary halt for Essex, but it didn't mean my cricket had stopped. Because on the Wednesday afternoon, I was off again ... to London Airport to catch the plane up to the North East, to play in the Rest of the World matches at Jesmond.

The match usually attracts interest but probably not as much as this time – because of guess who? That's right, Ian Botham's scheduled presence in the England side meant that the press coverage was considerable. It was to be Both's first match back after his suspension.

Some people might think that these games are just muck-abouts for the beer. Frankly, they couldn't be wider of the mark. OK, it's not ultra-serious cricket like a Test match. But with the calibre of people playing, you can't turn up and fool around because reputations are at stake. Make a fool of yourself in that class of company and your mates never let you forget it! And you couldn't complain at the cricket 'names' assembled by the Callers Pegasus company.

The Rest of the World XI, for whom I played, had the West Indian Test openers, Gordon Greenidge and Desmond Haynes, followed by people like Sunil Gavaskar, Richie Richardson, Roger Harper, Malcolm Marshall, Michael Holding and three of my old Aussie mates, Rodney Marsh, Dennis Lillee and Terry Alderman. England had players like Bill Athey, Allan Lamb, Keith Fletcher, Derek Pringle, Chris Smith, Kim Barnett, Richard Ellison and John Lever. Not a bad line-up, eh?

There were two centuries in that first match – Greenidge's 114 for us (I made 79 not out) and Lamb's 106 for England which threatened to win the match. But our 300 for six was enough in the end, England being bowled out for 268. Within the match, which was played incidentally before a capacity crowd of 4,000, there were any number of little cameo performances. Like Dennis Lillee slipping in the odd ball here and there at something resembling his old pace off a full length run-up, to his old adversary Keith Fletcher. Dennis gloved Keith with a short one which Fletch managed to get down to third man. As he ran past, Dennis told him: 'Sorry about that Fletch, but I just had to give you one for old time's sake.' Clearly, Dennis hadn't forgotten 1974 when he and Thommo sorted out England in that Ashes series which Australia won so well.

Watching Dennis bowl like that turned the clock back. He bowled off a short run generally and bowled well within himself. But he has still got good pace and control. Yet he probably hadn't bowled a ball for almost twelve months. Dennis said he was stiff and sore after that first day but he was still ready for more.

Marshie was enjoying it all because he had been nominated our captain. He lost no time in going into the England dressing room before the start and winding them up about how he was going to let all this terrific firepower loose on the English batsmen. His front line strike bowlers were Lillee, Marshall and Holding with Alderman and Harper to back them up. A pretty useful attack.

That first night, we had a marvellous evening; good food and wine, good conversation and lots of it. I hadn't seen Dennis and Rod for a while so we swapped a few tales. Good times.

Watching Rod Marsh in action behind the stumps, I could not escape the conclusion that, given a month's hard work, Marshie could be back in top grade cricket. And he wouldn't be out of place.

Now I don't know whether he would admit it, but I always had the feeling he quit too soon. When he packed up, I was surprised because he was still keeping magnificently, he was scoring the odd run – and quite honestly, there wasn't any reason to retire, other than the fact that his mates, like Greg Chappell and Dennis Lillee, had packed it up. I felt it was a shame Rod was influenced by that because in my book, he finished too soon.

All right, I accept he got out at the top and all that jazz. But when you have packed up, I just wonder whether you feel a year or two later: Hell, I did finish too quickly. I don't want to experience that. When I end my career, I really want to feel for evermore, it was the right time to quit. Not hanker after it a year or two later or even be forced to concede, I'd packed up too soon. So Marsh retired around the same time as his mates. But perhaps he was too hasty.

Honours finished even at Jesmond because England won the second game, on the Friday. Greenidge and myself again got some runs (he made 74, I got 61). But England passed our 276 total for the loss of seven wickets thanks mainly to Botham, who got 94. I'm pleased to say he fell to my lethal spin bowling, stumped by Marsh, as he was going for a seventh six which would have given him a ton! That showed Both it was for real – we couldn't have him getting a hundred in his come back game, could we?

Jesmond had been a lot of fun but it was time for myself and the rest of the Essex boys to head a long way south, right down to the English Channel, in fact, and Eastbourne. Essex were the first visitors of the week at the famous Saffrons ground and I was looking forward to it. It's a lovely ground, one I came across back in 1977 when I was with Gloucestershire Seconds. And it was Gloucestershire 'Firsts' who were uppermost in our minds as we flew back to London and then drove to Eastbourne that Friday night. Gloucestershire had stolen a march on us earlier that week, by beating Worcestershire and earning 20 points. Not even Graeme Hick's magnificent 134 (out of 234) could save Worcestershire. And victory put Gloucestershire 40 points clear at the top.

It wasn't time to panic – after all, this was only the first weekend of August coming up, and six weeks remained of the cricket season, time enough for us to harvest plenty of points. But a lead like that would require some catching and we all understood the importance of the Sussex match, particularly with Gloucestershire starting a week's cricket at the Cheltenham Festival. Two home games for them and the opportunity to extend their lead. The stakes were getting high. Nor could we forget two other counties which had climbed into the frame – Surrey and Hampshire. Nottinghamshire were not far behind, either, although they stood 14 points behind us and had played a game more. So they had a lot to do to catch Gloucestershire.

Maybe in a situation like this one, you can worry too much about what the other sides are doing. Generally, I believe in the principle that you can only get your own performance right and that's it. Either that will be enough or it won't be. But worrying about your opponents isn't terribly positive anyway and it doesn't do much good.

Whether we were thinking about the race for the Championship and importance of this match, I don't know. But we let Sussex off the hook on the Saturday morning at Eastbourne. We won the toss and put them in, hoping to extract some assistance from the wicket early on. We did, too – they were 39 for three and looking a bit shaky. We were on top, but 'were' was the operative word. Colin Wells came in and blazed away right from the word go. He made his first 50 in just 62 balls, 44 of them in boundaries. Wells and Neil Lenham put on 170 for the fourth wicket, Wells getting 106 and his partner 68. Then Garth Le Roux and Tony Pigott also got some, and Sussex ended up making 346 partly because we put down some fairly straightforward catches. By the close that night, we had lost Graham Gooch who made 31 out of 49 before Pigott had him leg before wicket.

The weather had been glorious all day and even when we finished, the sun was still shining strongly on a warm evening. Normally, I wouldn't get up to very much on a Saturday night, with a Sunday game to play. Just a few beers with the lads and then off to bed. But this time, I had the chance to see a little of the lovely countryside near Eastbourne – and it was a great evening. I went off with some friends to a delightful small pub, the Sussex Ox, near Alfriston in Sussex. It was only about ten minutes drive from Eastbourne along the coast but on such a lovely evening, it was magnificent. We followed the coast road and saw the Cuckmere Valley glittering in the evening sunshine, before turning inland along one of those lanes which seem to epitomize England.

Through the small hamlet of Litlington you come to the pub right under one of the hills of the South Downs. An idyllic spot. But it was no deserted country pub and that suggested they had something going for them at the place – the car park was choc-a-bloc. Maybe you have to grab the chance to go out in the summer evenings in England, when you can, I don't know. But plenty of people had come to this place, that's for sure. We had a steak cooked on the barbecue outside and it was superb. A great meal and a very pleasant evening before I drove back to the hotel.

It was a good thing we went on such a lovely night because the weather was a lot different the next morning. It rained heavily for a while and we had to make do with a twenty overs a side match in the Sunday League. Our 138 for seven was too much for Sussex who could manage only 99 for five. We were lucky – the rain washed out the attempts of Hampshire and Northamptonshire to play, so that we closed the gap between ourselves and the joint leaders to only four points. Hampshire, however, were well placed – they had a match in hand.

That Sunday match victory, however, was to be our only one of the visit to Eastbourne. Sussex set us some target in the fourth innings – 319 in what turned out to be 49 overs. I don't know whether we should have taken it as a compliment to our batting ability or what! But Ian Gould certainly wasn't playing the Father Christmas role, was he?

In the end, however, we got very close to it. We needed 156 from the last hour and I was still there. But I always felt it was just beyond us even though we gave it all we could. I finished on 108 not out but it wasn't my greatest knock of the summer. In that situation, you get in there and get on with it. Sometimes it comes off, sometimes it doesn't. But I'd have certainly sacrificed a personal ton for a victory, especially when we heard that Gloucestershire had turned the match against Hampshire at Cheltenham upside down. Hampshire only needed 116 to win, but folded for 98. And after all I said about them – there's thanks for you!

It all meant Gloucestershire were a huge 54 points ahead at the top of the table. And our great dream of becoming County Champions looked in real trouble.

The defeat set Hampshire back. And as Surrey had still played a game more than us, they had a lot to do. It suddenly started to look as though we might be the only ones who could catch the West Country club. And even our chances didn't look too bright.

I'd had another disappointment, too, at this time. My original plans to play all season had altered by the news that the Australians were going to fit in a tour of India, before England arrived in Australia to prepare for the Ashes series. That meant I had to go home early – and the date I had set was 22 August. I had tried to stay longer because that wasn't the date the tour began in India. But the Australian authorities told me that I would have to go into training camp with the team, before we set off for India. That meant flying halfway across the world back to Brisbane, then coming halfway back again, to India. I can't say I was thrilled by the idea.

Then my arrangements changed again. I had thought my last game would be the County Championship match against Gloucestershire at Colchester, finishing on 22 August. I was to fly home that night immediately after the match. And the way the race for the Championship was boiling up, it looked like a great match to play in as a final game for Essex. Don't get me wrong – I was still desperately disappointed not to be staying until the end of the season. Those final weeks were going to be vital and with England playing the Final Test against New Zealand at The Oval on the Thursday and Friday of that Gloucestershire match, we were sure to miss some key players like Goochie and others perhaps. But then came news that the Australians had fitted in an extra match in India. And because of it, they would have to leave home a few days earlier. My schedule, therefore, had to be brought forward – and I realized I had to fly home on the eve of the Gloucestershire match. To say I was bitterly disappointed would be an under statement.

All I could do, I felt, was play as well as I could possibly do until then. And I would have to hope the lads could catch Gloucestershire themselves. I felt, in a way, I was letting them down. Maybe that was silly because they understood the situation. And all the Essex people were terrific about it when I told them. Their attitude was magnificent.

So we went back to Chelmsford and had a good match against Middlesex. We batted first and got 382 for eight declared. Keith Fletcher scored 91, another fine innings, and Alan Lilley made 87. Middlesex were then shot out for 116 and, following on 266 behind, finished the second day at 142 for five. Only Wilf Slack held us up and his 89 not out confirmed for me that England had given him short shrift too soon.

Slack couldn't save his side the next day; in fact, he only added another four runs. They were all out for 174 leaving us winners by an innings and 92 runs. The 24 points were most welcome, especially when news came through that Nottinghamshire had ended Gloucestershire's run of five successive wins, in a drawn match at Cheltenham. Gloucestershire took only 5 points, closing the gap between us to 35 points. Still we had two games in hand.

It had been a busy week and a thoroughly important one. At least at the end of it, we knew that we were right back in the title hunt. Our great dream had not yet died.

13

The last lap

There were just ten days left of my only season in English County cricket as I walked out to bat against Leicestershire at Leicester on 9 August. Ten days and only two County Championship matches, plus two Sunday League games. It all seemed to have gone so quickly now that I was on the verge of finishing my season. But if I had harboured images of grandeur in those final few games, a tall, skinny fast bowler by the name of Jonathan Agnew ('Aggers' to everyone) had other plans.

We had won the toss and taken first knock. But 43 for two was not promising and my fall two runs later for a duck hardly helped matters. I was very disappointed. Brian Hardie, Neil Foster and Alan Lilley stuck around for a while but 216 all out didn't look too hot to me, particularly with Leicestershire 55 for two at the close. But a strange thing was to happen in the game before it was over.

Before that, we beat Leicestershire by 24 runs in the Sunday League, to move into joint second place. The weather only allowed 18 overs a side but Hardie's superb 80 helped us to 151 for three and Leicestershire could manage only 127 for eight. Events elsewhere conspired to assist us, too. Hampshire lost to Sussex at Bournemouth on a faster scoring rate and at Wellingborough, Northamptonshire ran into a whirlwind called Botham who smashed 175 not out including a record 13 sixes. What a score, what a player. Were there still really people in England who felt he shouldn't be brought back into the Test side? I couldn't imagine so.

Northants took two points from that match against Somerset

because the rain stopped play for the day after only 15 overs of their innings. But I reckon they counted themselves a shade fortunate to take two points, because 272 for five off 39 overs, looked some score to try and beat. So Northants led by two points with Hampshire and ourselves locked in second place on 34 points. It wasn't only the Championship which was warming up on the last lap.

The rain which had wrecked much of the Sunday League hung around the next day. So it wasn't until Tuesday morning that we could start again at Leicester. And by then, things had been happening. . .under the covers!

We had been lucky, it turned out, to bat first. Because in the normal course of events, if it had been a bright sunny day on the Monday, I have a feeling the wicket would have played very well and Leicestershire might have got 350. That would have put them in the box seat – almost 150 in front with time to bowl us out. But what happened was that a certain amount of moisture probably got under the mat during our 18 overs for the silly season game! And on the Monday, with the mat still covering the Saturday wicket, the moisture remained underneath. The following morning, the two captains got together so they declared at 55 and, in 18 overs, we made 159. None of their bowlers were regulars – it was a real 'gimme' all right!

Leicestershire needed 320 to win. But Peter Willey probably didn't realize there would be that much moisture in the track. After all, you couldn't tell from our batting in the second innings because it was against non-bowlers. So Leicestershire found Foster seaming the ball around and they slid to 69 for six. We had a tremendous spell just before and after lunch, pushing them from 48 for one to 69 for six. We felt it was just a matter of mopping up the tail from then on.

It should have been, too. Except that yours truly put a spoke in that particular wheel by dropping De Freitas when they were still in the seventies. And that seemed to sustain them. That dropped catch broke the spell we had over them, something I had seen before in cricket games. You are enjoying a great run of getting wickets and suddenly someone drops a catch. That seems to buck up the batting side and they mount a rearguard defence. Which is precisely what Leicestershire did now.

If I had taken that catch, I felt they would have been all out for less than 100. But I've dropped many catches in the past and I'll drop them in the future. You never like dropping them especially if you've got a side on the roll. You like to maintain it.

De Freitas made 22, Whitticase got 55 not out and Agnew made 21. Sixty-nine for six became 146 for seven. But eventually we got them out, for 190, with Foster taking five for 84. We picked up 18 points and really cheered when we heard Middlesex had beaten Gloucestershire. It meant the gap between us was down to 19 points – and still we had those two games in hand.

Leicestershire have a good side, there is no doubt of that. Their medium pace and quick bowling is very handy. There is De Freitas, Taylor, Agnew and Benjamin, who is an overseas player and they also have Ferris, another overseas man. Paddy Clift is a thoroughly useful all-rounder. But I suspect they missed Nick Cook this season. Peter Willey will bowl well for you but he won't run through a side. If Cook was still on the staff they would have a tremendous bowling attack.

When David Gower is in the side, it looks a thoroughly impressive team. And what of James Whitaker, who was to end the season with a place in the England squad for the tour of Australia? Well, he didn't do that well against us, making just five runs in the second innings. But it's not fair to judge on that performance in the light of his terrific season overall. Maybe he will find next season tougher, that is possible. When you have such a successful year, it is always hard to sustain that the following season. But he certainly looks to be a quality batsman.

Making arrangements for the long journey home filled my next few days. It was the usual scenario – seeing friends for the last time, getting things packed. It seemed to take us right through to the final weekend. We did not have a midweek game starting on the Wednesday because of the Nat West Bank Trophy semi-finals. So I had the chance to see Trevor Jesty's brave knock for Surrey which so nearly put his County in the final. But not quite . . .

Saturday was sunny – and Northants made the most of winning the toss at Colchester. They didn't start that well, with Cook and Boyd-Moss soon out. But Allan Lamb's fine 81 and 63 from Robert Bailey pushed them to 302. But from our point of view, although we had been sorry not to win the toss and bat first because we suspected the wicket might be more difficult later on in the game, it wasn't a bad start. Neil Foster took five wickets in an innings for the tenth time in the season, finishing with five for 83. There was no doubt that our Championship challenge had revived partly due to Foster's fine spell of bowling in recent weeks. Of course, others played their part. Any successful side needs that. But Foster had bowled well recently as his figures indicated. And by the close on the Saturday night, with Graham Gooch 40 not out in a total of 56 for one, we seemed well enough placed. After all, we had achieved our first target – maximum bowling points.

That evening, the boys gave me a party at Keith Fletcher's place. They were all there and they presented me with a silver platter with all their signatures on, to commemorate my season with Essex. It was a great gesture and a real surprise – I hadn't been 'in' on the secret, for obvious reasons. I thoroughly enjoyed a memorable evening.

Perhaps the beers we sank that night helped us the next day because by Sunday night we were out on our own at the top of the Sunday League. Northants, the leaders at that point, couldn't stop Brian Hardie – he made a super 109 out of 234 for five. My last Sunday League score wasn't that memorable – 25. But our victory was far more important than my personal score. Northants made 202 for nine so we won by 32 runs and went to the top because Hampshire lost to Middlesex at Lord's. More than halfway through August – it was a good time to go to the top of the Sunday League table. Maybe we could do the same in the Championship.

The benefit of hindsight will tell you of the dramas which were just around the corner in this match. But there were few signs of them as we made 337 on the second day of the Championship game. Three players made half centuries – Gooch with 87, Prichard with 72 and Hardie, 66. Northants, at 36 for one, were one run ahead at the close.

My 28 wasn't exactly what I had planned for my final Championship game. Maybe 128 would have been nearer the idea I had in mind. But Nick Cook helped decree otherwise. His four for 76 off 32 overs, plus Roger Harper's one for 52 in 24 overs indicated the ball was turning, albeit slowly. But the die was cast. And the headline in one of the national daily newspapers on the last morning of the game, the Tuesday, was to turn out somewhat prophetic. 'Spinners could hold up Essex in run chase' it said. How right it was to be, only the spinners did rather more than just hold us up. They flattened us, to be quite honest!

The man who gave us no doubts whatever as to the task we would face in the fourth innings, was one of our own men – Charlie Childs. He took his best return for Essex – eight for 61 off 30.2

overs. It was a bad omen for us as Northants were bowled out for 181, leaving us 146 to win.

I've got to be honest – I felt 150 on that wicket was sufficient a target to make us struggle. It was not easy batting on it, but it wasn't impossible. But I felt we had a chance to make the 140-odd for victory.

What happened was that we played really badly on it and they bowled really well. But all out for 44 – it was a dreadful way to end my career with Essex. The wicket had started to play up well before the final day, for the bounce was irregular. But 44? Ridiculous!

Every shot became a dismissal, just about. And there was rank bad batting. I include myself in that. I also blame myself for failing twice and I suspect it may have been partly because, deep down, I was thinking about home by then. I knew I had to rush straight off from the ground to the house, get things loaded up and then go straight to the airport. I should have been thinking of nothing but the cricket – but I wasn't altogether.

Yet I really wanted to go out on a high note. I would have loved a win in my final game. I felt a bit unlucky to get out in the first innings by dragging the ball on to my stumps. I had been trying to run the ball down past the slips but got an edge and pulled the ball on to my wicket. Just one of those bad shots. But in the second innings, I just played over the top of a ball. It wasn't a memorable end by any means, I'm afraid to say.

The papers called it 'The flop of the season'. And I suppose they were right. After such a good run in recent matches, it was a lousy end to my season, I can tell you. It was the lowest score any side had made in the Championship for almost three seasons. But against that, you would have to say the turn the spinners were getting was pretty phenomenal. The wicket just didn't last as a first-class wicket.

Amazingly, we had been 13 without loss. And then 31 for two. So 44 was really crazy after that opening. Cook got five for 14 in 16 overs and Mallender four for 22. Our second highest scorer was 'Extras' with ten. What a shambles.

Yet believe it or not, we still closed the gap at the top again because Gloucestershire picked up only three points from their defeat by Warwickshire. And as we had earned maximum bonus points at Colchester – eight – we were now only 14 points adrift of them, with two matches in hand. Some consolation? I suppose it ought to have been. But there really isn't any sort of consolation to be gleaned from the wreckage of 44 all out. Especially when you are going flat out for the County Champions title. I shall not remember it as much of an occasion, my last day of cricket with Essex.

The match was all over by four o'clock so I wasn't rushing any more. I had time to get home, change and sort out last minute things before leaving for Heathrow. The British Airways people again looked after us very well and away we went.

I got home feeling tired, inevitably, but enriched by the experience. Yet there was a sense of unfinished business. Even as the flight home was continuing, I pictured the lads going out to face Gloucestershire the next day, in what could be the most vital match of the summer. It could decide the destiny of the title. I wished I was still there with them, making better scores than 28 and 6, the ones from my last game. That was a big disappointment and no sort of send off at all. About as good as flat beer, in fact!

Perhaps that last match, from my own point of view, summed up the whole summer. It had been an in and out season for me – very much so, in fact. The final aggregate will tell you that my batting figures in first-class cricket read as follows: matches, 20; innings, 32; not outs, 4; highest score, 150; runs, 1385; average, 49.46. I was to finish thirteenth in the national batting averages and the highest placed Essex batsman.

My summary of all that? Not brilliant. All right, I scored almost 1,400 runs and maybe to some people that sounds good. But it is when I score my runs that motivates me nowadays more than just the fact that if you look at the final figures, they seem OK. In fact, they don't always tell the true story. I made a couple of hundreds in second innings situations, like the one against Surrey at The Oval; situations where we just had to bat out for a draw. So those innings did not play any significant part in the game, other than helping us save them each time. I got 150 down at Glamorgan which was fair but their attack was a little bit weak, also, it was a very flat track. The innings that I played which really meant something to me were the ones such as the 50-odd not out I made at Lord's against Middlesex when we won the game. It was an important innings. Even the hundred I made against Sussex at Eastbourne was just a bludgeoning sort of slog. I could have got out at any time but I ended up getting a hundred. Little merit in that, in my book.

In the one-day games especially, early in the season, I had chances to win games for Essex or certainly put us in a stronger position, but I wasn't playing particularly well and failed quite often. In my analysis, I felt I had one of those seasons where on some days I played well and felt good but the next day, for some reason, it eluded me. I don't feel Essex saw the best of me at all and for that I'm sorry. That is the one thing which disappointed me more than any other single factor.

I know you cannot have it your own way the whole time. But I always like to go out and play a certain way and anything under that sort of standard, I don't really think I have performed well. Maybe I'm being a little bit harsh on myself because sometimes you come up against some good bowling, you get a good ball, the wicket plays up on you a little bit or something happens that is not totally your fault. But I still feel I did not really play as well as I know I could have done. So that has to be the disappointment of it all because I think maybe Essex could have done better in the Benson and Hedges or Nat West one-day knock-out competitions, had I played a greater part.

I had wanted to play a final at Lord's. That was always a great ambition in the back of my mind. But when the chance came to make a decisive contribution, I couldn't come up with the goods, against either Nottinghamshire in the Benson and Hedges or Warwickshire in the Nat West. A pity. But both important knock-out games were at times when I wasn't playing particularly well. You get disappointments in cricket and you have to accept them. You have no choice. But I'll always feel sorry I didn't play in a one-day final at Lord's for Essex. That would have been marvellous. A bad case, I'm afraid, of 'if only'. But then life cannot be like that, can it?

14

My team-mates in close-up

Around twenty-six hours on an aeroplane heading for Australia gave me plenty of time to mull over some thoughts on the English County cricket scene. I looked back and reflected on a summer which had contained a great many unpredictabilities, surprises and disappointments. At the end of it all I felt I had learned a great deal, both as a cricketer and as an ordinary person. It was an experience I shall always remember.

The standard of English County cricket, in my view, is very high indeed. Every side can beat any other on a given day, given a good performance by their star players or even just some of the lesser known players chipping in doing something particularly good.

The final result of the season, Glamorgan beating Essex at Chelmsford, proved the point. By then, of course, Essex had won that prized County Championship title – and I was thrilled when the news reached me, during Australia's tour of India. I raised a few glasses of beer that night in celebration – it was great news. Even though I was thousands of miles away from all the excitement and celebrations, I was happy to feel I had played a small part in it. It is history now, of course, but Essex almost beat Gloucestershire, their last pair holding out for a draw after Charlie Childs had taken eight wickets in Gloucestershire's first innings. That must have been particularly sweet for Charlie because Gloucestershire were the county which let him go. Charlie's revenge! And even with a draw, Essex cut the gap between the two teams to eleven points. Subsequent victories as Gloucestershire stumbled gave Essex their fourth Championship title in eight years – a record they should be proud of. A great achievement.

Looking at the season overall from an Australian's viewpoint, I was particularly struck by the realization that there are no such things as easy runs in County cricket except in the declaration-type situation. You've always got to contend with a more than useful fast bowler who is invariably moving the ball around or a very tidy medium pace attack. There are some good spinners, too, bowlers like Eddie Hemmings, Pat Pocock, Charlie Childs, Phil Edmonds, John Emburey and Nick Cook. Balancing that is the fact that every side has some good young batsmen so it is a very healthy competition. As far as the English players are concerned, they are definitely stronger in batting than bowling. And the overseas players are primarily responsible for that. If you added up how many wickets fell in a County season and what percentage was taken by overseas as against English bowlers, it would provide an indictment of English bowling. As well as the overseas guys there are players like Mortensen, Connor and Curran who are not yet qualified to play for England.

There is no end in sight to the situation because so many Counties have now started to introduce a new practice. I don't know that you can call it flouting the rules but maybe it would be classed as against the spirit of the laws and certainly the TCCB's campaign to get more players who are eligible for England playing in the County sides. The situation in which Counties have two overseas players on their books mean that they back each other up, week after week. Several Counties have this arrangement – Kent, with Eldine Baptiste and Terry Alderman, Surrey with Tony Gray and Sylvester Clarke, Lancashire with Clive Lloyd and Patrick Patterson and Leicestershire with George Ferris and Winston Benjamin. Warwickshire have Anton Ferreira and Brian McMillan. So instead of really burning out one player over twenty-four County Championship matches and all the one-day games, these players take it in turns so that they get about twelve Championship games each or more one-day games to balance it up. They are able to burn in at full stretch for that game they play in, knowing they have got the next week off. And if they do happen to get any sort of injury, they can be treated and don't have to rush back.

I don't see that situation as one conducive to the healthy future of English cricket. I've got to admit that. In my view, it is extending the problem from what it might have been in the past. It begins to look as though some Counties will always try to find a way around certain rulings. And there are other aspects to it which some would find disturbing.

Finances, for a start, must play a part. The wealthier Counties automatically have an advantage because they can afford to pay two overseas stars and keep them comparatively fresh. But poorer Counties could never afford two stars so they have to make do with one guy. And if he gets injured and is out of action for six weeks, that's just tough luck. Not an ideal arrangement, is it?

Another point, which I have mentioned before, is that if overseas stars are not burning themselves out in County cricket, they are even fresher for their countries when they play for them. They're getting the best of both worlds – they are still in the learning environment but without all the heavy physical work which can wear players out quickly, especially bowlers. Ideal for guys like Patrick Patterson and Tony Gray, the latter player who I am sure will become a major strike bowler with the West Indies in the years ahead.

The situation as a whole is hard to legislate against if Counties are determined to find a way around the rules. All the TCCB can do is try and encourage Counties to bring on their own young players as much as they can, particularly the spinners. I believe people get sick and tired of seeing fast bowlers rushing in hour after hour. OK, it is exciting to see a fast bowler in action. For a while. But not all day. You do like to see a spinner operating at the other end, plying his trade. The relentless pace barrage can be a bit boring.

Nor am I sure that having all these overseas players is always the way to be successful. Admittedly, I played for Essex this season – but not in the last month of the season when Essex wrapped up the Championship. The guys did it on their own in those vital late matches. And all credit to them. Anyway, Essex only had one overseas player. Counties with more than one overseas player, like Lancashire, Kent, Surrey and Warwickshire, didn't win anything this season.

On another theme, I felt that the few spinners around who did thrive in County cricket had to be pretty useful performers to exist. Perhaps the lbw rules need to be looked at again. But certainly players play spin a lot better than they used to and spinners have to be pretty good to survive.

If you analyse it, lbw should mean just leg before wicket. There seem to be too many rules nowadays about hitting outside the line and striking the pad in the line of the wicket, pitched outside leg, too far forward and all this sort of thing. Frankly, I believe it clouds the issue. I would like to see them do something about the ball pitching outside leg stump. The only danger is that you might get negative type bowling if you changed the ruling, with bowlers firing into patches outside your leg stump.

Maybe Ray Illingworth would not agree with this, but players use their pad and bat a lot better nowadays than they used to, rather than playing out at the ball and then taking the chance of it hitting the edge of the bat, perhaps via a pad, to a close fielder. Players play a lot tighter now.

In a sense, it is a grey area of the play. But you should feel comforted by the fact that in England you have the best umpires in the world. One or two of the funniest, too, if you think of people like Dickie Bird, one of the great characters of the game.

The reason the English umpires are so good is that they are professionals. Almost all of them seem to have played first-class cricket at some stage of their careers and because of that you tend to get a better decision maker. In other countries, you get guys who just have a love for the game. They go into umpiring and learn all the rules and regulations but sometimes they don't understand the pressures and goings on like a former player would. Therefore, that can cloud their decisions.

English umpires still make mistakes, just like anyone else in the world. After all, they are human, aren't they? And I don't have any complaint about that situation. But speaking personally, I have got far more confidence in English officials and the vast majority of umpires over here are as good as anywhere in the world.

On the subject of umpires at international level, I believe we are heading in the direction of neutral umpires in all Test matches. And I feel it would be a good thing on the whole. What happens a lot now in Test series is that it seems to be an easy way out to go home and blame the umpire for losing. But that isn't right, it can't be.

Already in other sports, such as Rugby Union and Rugby League, you have neutral referees. For the 1985 Australia–New Zealand Rugby Union series, in New Zealand, a Welsh referee handled the first two Tests and a Scot flew out for the third. It won't change the referee – sometimes he will have a good game, sometimes a bad one. Again, he is only human. But at least he is totally neutral and there is nothing you can moan about. Having neutral officials would take that factor out of the game. And cricket would be the better for its absence. But raising standards is not an easy thing to do. In Australia, for example, most umpires work nine to five in offices and just umpire for a pastime. It is basically like anything else – you just get better with experience.

Cricket players could help create better umpires too – I would like to see them give umpires more of a break. Now if that sounds strange coming from a player I would say that there shouldn't be a brick wall between players and officials. There ought to be trust, understanding and such qualities. These days cricket becomes very emotional, very tense and pressure is placed on umpires. Too much in my view – I believe unfairly so. We're all guilty of it – and we ought to put our hands up and admit it. You all appeal for things which you know basically are not out. It's just that you get caught up in the excitement of things. So if there is a little nick down legside or the ball bumps off the pad, you catch it and yell for it. But immediately after you've done it – and this can apply even if a player is given out – you get into a bit of a huddle and you might say: 'Gee, I didn't think that was out.' You feel you have got that one, sort of thing.

Then, if one is given not out that you think is out, you make a ruck about it. But I believe it is like anything – you have got to be able to accept the good with the bad. It's not always easy to do but it has to be done. Maybe the players have got to try and realize that a little bit better.

The TV screens have got to be fairer to umpires, too. They don't escape in my criticism. They slow down these run-outs, they can freeze-frame it and sometimes the batsman is six inches out which looks quite a lot on a TV screen. You say: 'Well there's the line and there's the end of the bat – he was out.' But look at it in normal speed, under pressure with arms and legs going everywhere. Frankly, I don't envy an umpire his job having to make decisions in those circumstances. It would be very very difficult. So if they make a mistake, I believe the TV should be less harsh in its analysis. Why? Because it is all very well for the experts to sit up there in the air-conditioned comfort of a commentary position and make statements about bad umpiring or bad cricket, etc. But the game out in the middle is a lot harder than it would seem. The decisions they make are split second jobs and they are tough.

If there is any 'stick' to be handed out, I'll be prepared to cop my fair share of it. I'm not blameless. But although I admit I have rucked about umpiring decisions, I think when you get older you start to realize that it is a pretty difficult job they have. I'm pleased to say that generally speaking, I enjoy a chat with umpires and I get on with them. That's how it should be. Courtesy, after all, costs nothing, does it?

That is one memory of the English County circuit I shall keep with me for a long time – the camaraderie of it all. Cricket is a very friendly game in England at County level and I liked that a lot. OK, you have your moments when it becomes tense and you get the odd show of temper. But who in the world never shows a flash of temper or irritation at his work? I'm happy to say it is rare in County cricket, from my experience, at least. The game is played in an excellent spirit and yet it is throughly competitive. I liked that.

Essex, for example, were a very competitive side. But we played the game in the right way and I hope people see it in that light. Because the fact that Essex have been so successful in recent seasons proves beyond doubt that you can be pleasant and mix a competitive edge with courtesy, while still finishing up winners. I'm not in favour of the view in any sport that you've got to be nasty to win – I just don't go along with that at all.

Maybe I would have liked to have been a bit younger when I experienced the County scene, and perhaps played a bit more. But these things come along in life at times when you cannot know. I never really had an approach from an English County before. Now whether that was my fault for not showing an interest, I don't know. I would say I would never have written to Counties asking if they were interested in me. But when the approach came from Essex, I was glad to accept. And if it had come five years ago, I probably would have done the same. I do admit I would like to have been about twenty-five and played five years of County cricket. It would have been great. Still, I have enjoyed the experience even though it was only for one season. I'm happy I did it.

I made my decision to play only one season with Essex once I knew I had to go to India. Another nine months of straight cricket was staring me in the face. But I admit I wasn't clear about it in my mind. I worried that I would have a month off at home after the Australian summer and then start getting itchy feet again and wanting to play cricket. I'm not one for lazing around for very long – I like to keep active generally.

That happened last time I had a winter off. That was after the West Indies tour in 1984 and it was a break of four months or so. When it came to August, I found it hard to get back into cricket. I was lackadaisical about getting fit again and getting into the swing of things.

Usually it has been a lot better when I've only had a short break. I have enjoyed that more. I fear that around next May I will be at home in Brisbane, working with Castlemaine and having time to play with the kids and relax much more... but then my mind will drift over to England and Essex. I'll start to think: I could have been over there with the boys. I'll keep in touch, obviously, and by July I may well feel I should have come back for another season.

I do expect to miss it because you build up a certain number of friendships. And I enjoyed the Essex way of doing things and the people I was involved with. I know I need a break from the game but I'm not sure whether five months will be too much. Only time will tell.

I admit, just as August began, I was tempted to ask Essex if I could go back on my decision not to come back. I felt: Oh hell, I'll cancel that and ask to stay another year after all. I wanted to play in a Lord's final, as I said, but I also very much wanted to be in the team for that final game when Essex clinch a title, whether it be the Championship or the Sunday League. That feeling of being in the winner's dressing room is a really special one. Missing out on Essex winning the Championship was a major disappointment to me. And as I wouldn't be at all surprised to see them retain the title next summer, I know what I could be missing.

The only thing which makes me think it was the right decision not to stay another year was my uncertainty – and, add to that, my feelings for my family. It will be good for them to be settled and lead a normal family existence for those months, with Dad at home, rather than being on their own for so long or transporting everything and everyone across the world once again. I know kids are adaptable but there is a limit to what you can ask at times! But having said that, I'll never tire of coming back to England. It is like a home away from home really for Jane and me. We have got similar ideas on things, our two countries, we enjoy the same sort of lifestyle. OK, the climate is a bit different (that's a diplomatic way of putting it, isn't it?), but I always enjoy being here. So I'll be back some day and probably quite soon.

151

You could say I was influenced in my decision to have a season off by the example of other players, like Ian Botham and Joel Garner. They both had seasons away from the game, missing overseas tours. They felt they had to have some time away from cricket and I fully understand that feeling. It is a bit hard to explain. It is not as if you are not enjoying it – you are, and yet you feel you are not operating at full potential. The snap, the spark isn't quite as bright as it was and as it should be. The lifestyle is great and there is nothing wrong with the game. But you feel saturated with it all, especially if you are an international cricketer. I sometimes wonder if people realize just how much pressure top-class cricketers are under. They expect a brilliant century or a nine wicket haul by bowlers almost every time they go out to play, particularly if it is a Test match. Yet no one can produce that sort of form in every match, it is impossible.

Standards are demanded but although you always do your absolute best, there is never any guarantee, there cannot be, that you'll get a ton. Life just doesn't work that way. Sometimes an extended break is just the thing to re-charge tired batteries. It is as though the absolute pleasure has started to go away a little and it becomes just like a job. You start going through the motions too much, rather than being really excited about being out there. Often, too, the tension and pressure starts to get to you more if you are tired. So much tension is placed on you in international cricket. And as captain I find it even greater pressure than if I was just a player.

I have had six or seven straight years of non-stop cricket-playing and I fear it has diluted my enthusiasm for the game a little. That's nothing to worry about – I know a break will cure that. But without it, I'm not sure what it would do to my game, my enthusiasm for playing. And I didn't want to get halfway through a season with Essex and want to get on the first plane home because I was so tired. So I felt deep down I had to tell them I couldn't come back even if part of me was inclined to take a gamble and say: 'Go for it!' I know that when I return after my break, I'll return to cricket bursting with enthusiasm.

As for 1986 and Essex, I still ponder whether my form in the summer of 1986 was due to mental tiredness or just the comparison with 1985 and that Australian tour. I come down slightly on the side of the latter. I had such a good 1985 that I suppose I found what every player experiences – you have to come down to earth, so as to speak, at some stage.

You cannot expect to go out there and score the amount of runs I got in 1985 for ever and ever. You are bound to have periods where things don't go your way. Perhaps the problem is that people expect that form to continue for ever. I can only tell them through personal experience – it does not, it cannot. Believe me.

I thought I might sign off my season with Essex with an analysis of my team-mates, the guys who lifted the County Championship in my season with them, 1986. I feel that the great feeling of having played for the English Champion County in 1986 will take time to sink in but it's a wonderful thought. There was no domestic one-day final at Lord's for us, but the Championship has to be the top competition and therefore the most coveted. We all played a part but what impressed me probably more than anything else was the way Essex overcame adversity to win that title.

Look at the obvious 'name' players in the side – they didn't have the greatest of seasons. Neither Graham Gooch nor myself hit our top form. And look at the Essex players who represented England during the summer, often leaving the County side badly weakened ... Graham Gooch, Derek Pringle, Neil Foster and John Lever. So the guys left behind had to fill in a lot of holes and they did that superbly well, on the whole.

What of the future for Essex? Well, they have had ten great years but the good times have to come to an end at some stage. They may struggle for a certain amount of time and that could be just around the corner. But the lean periods won't last for long because they have a good base of young cricketers coming through. And the Essex way is sure to create a good team spirit, so I don't believe Essex's bad times will last, if and when they come.

You might not always win titles, but it is worth remembering that is not always the ultimate success. A successful side is a consistent side and occasionally you pick up these titles along the way. And all the while you provide entertainment for supporters and crowds all over the country and your players gain enormous pleasure from their time with the County. That is what it is all about.

Some people have wondered what I learned from being with Essex. Well the experience has taught me a lot. Watching blokes like Keith Fletcher go about his duties as skipper when Gooch was away and all that involved – that is making decisions, giving judgements, handling players in the right way to get the best out of them – has been highly beneficial to me. Through it, my own philosophical approach towards the game has changed quite a lot. In the past, I have been quite an intense player, prone to moods. But from my time with Essex, I have learned to accept the good times and the bad times and not become so morose when things don't go according to plan. It has been an education for me.

I have mentioned, probably quite a few times, something I term the Essex way. I'll tell you what I mean by that. It involves the spirit in the dressing room, the camaraderie and the support the team gets from the people of Essex. Some Counties might have internal strife or suffer through lack of support. But Essex are a tremendously well-supported County. OK, success breeds that but there are still other Counties which have been reasonably successful but still don't get the support which Essex enjoys. And that is down to the way they play the game. They are an enjoyable side to watch and there are always little sidelines apart from the actual batting and bowling and fielding. There is always some skylarking about at the right time; Keith Pont on a bicycle, Brian Hardie doing something or other, Keith Fletcher cracking a joke. The chit chat between the players out on the field is quite humorous at times.

The guys have been a real lot of fun to play cricket with. So, for better or worse, here are my thoughts about the cricketers whom I played alongside in the team which was to become English County Champions in 1986!

Graham Gooch By his standards, it was a disappointing season. He made two hundreds for England and hit a purple patch for Essex later in the summer. But it wasn't the same convincing, all-conquering Goochie which we have come to expect. Why? I don't really know but I suspect it could have been a follow-on from the West Indies tour problems. Perhaps the winter Graham has had in England having a break from cricket will have solved the problem. I believe it will do so and 1987 will see Graham back to his very best.

As regards the captaincy, Graham picked up where Keith Fletcher left off. And I believe he could be a very good captain. As far as the textbook goes, if you follow that, he does all those things correctly. The only trouble with Graham is that he is such an important part of the team just as a batsman. And that can mean when he goes through periods of depression like we all do if we're not playing particularly well, you tend to get caught up in your own game a little bit. And then you forget about your captaincy duties. Maybe that happened a couple of times but he will learn from it.

He has already learned the value of Keith's style of leadership in taking guys aside for a quiet word as soon as there are any dramas. Graham has basically learned the Fletcher approach to captaincy and if he follows that I don't believe he will go far wrong.

Keith Fletcher He would have to be as good a captain as I have played with or against. He follows a certain pattern of leadership in terms of bowling changes or field placings. He seems to have an uncanny knack of putting a guy in the right spot at the right time. Now that can be interpreted as luck, but in his case, I would say it's because he has been around such a long time and knows the players so well, both his own and the opposing team's guys.

I would say the biggest thing I have learned from him is the way he manages people. He has a great rapport with the players and they have a hell of a lot of respect for him. They seem to give that little bit extra to him and that is probably why Essex have done so well because he has been able to keep the side in a very harmonious situation. There have been no real disputes.

Everyone seems to want to 'die' for Essex, and Fletcher has to have had a major influence on their thinking. I hope I have taken back to Australia those lessons Keith gave me during the summer. I can get down in the dumps a bit easily or get a bit critical, not spending enough time with the younger players in a one-to-one situation. But watching Keith, I have seen him grab one of the younger players if he's had a bad day and have a bit of a chat with the guy in the corner away from everyone else. Little bits and pieces like that I have observed and you only have to look at what Fletch has done for Essex in recent years to see the success of the man's approach.

Nor is Keith any sort of a passenger in the side. Even at his age, he makes the runs and makes them when they're needed. You only have to look at his contribution to the side this season. He can still make big scores.

David East He has had a disappointing year for him with the bat. He got more runs late in the summer including a ton. And he was still doing a good job behind the stumps. I spent a lot of time standing at second slip during the summer and Eastie hardly missed anything behind the wicket. If a 'keeper looks brilliant but misses chances all over the place, that is not what you want. So although Eastie might sometimes look untidy, you can bet that if a batsman nicks the ball, the Essex 'keeper will grab it. Also he made some good stumpings, so that was another good part of his work. I believe he is as good as Bruce French and that if you just want a good job done he is as good as anyone around. He also seems as though he is potentially a better bat than most of the other contenders. I feel that if he had enjoyed a better season with the bat, he might well have got a trip to Australia with England during the winter.

John 'Charlie' Childs Charlie has had a tremendous season. He says he thought his career was finished when he left Gloucestershire but Essex snapped him up and persevered with him when he had a poor first season. In 1986 he reaped the rewards of all the hard work he put in during the winter. What he did this summer in terms of the high wicket haul, was a real coup for Essex. They took him on when no one else wanted him and stuck by him. Once again, their fine judgement was proved correct. And Charlie still has a lot of good years left in him. He has such tremendous control now, that is the secret of his success. I think he has learned from the times he has bowled the ball a little too high because he has been punished. But he has shown a willingness to learn.

When he does bowl tightly, he is certainly one of the better spin bowlers around the County scene, now. He would be one of the only ones you would consider for the Test Match arena if players like Edmonds and Emburey were injured – Charlie or Eddie Hemmings, perhaps. I'm thoroughly pleased for Charlie about what happened this season because he is a really nice bloke. I remembered him from my stint down at Gloucestershire but I have to say he wasn't the dangerous bowler at that time, that he certainly was for Essex this summer.

David Acfield He might be at the veteran stage but no one should underestimate his ability as a spin bowler, even now. He is still very useful even in one-day cricket. Over the years and with the advent of limited-overs cricket he has probably become flatter in his bowling style. But there is no disputing his effectiveness. I think he bluffs people that he can't bat to save his life. He can rather more than he lets on. When 'Ackers' comes out, bowlers tend to lick their lips and think: This guy is easy meat. But it is amazing how he can hang in there and support a guy at the other end.

David proves that slow bowlers do still have a place in one-day sides. To my way of thinking, unless a guy is an exceptional medium pacer who can bat well or a very, very fast bowler who is superbly accurate, then the spinners are one of your most important weapons of one-day cricket. If a slow bowler bowls well in limited-overs cricket, he can really get among the wickets bowling in the middle of an innings just when a side is trying to get on with the scoring. If you go into a match with an all medium pace attack, you have no variety if that type of bowling is being hit. If a spinner is hit, the batsman has to hit him pretty straight most of the time whereas if a quick bowler is hit, the snicks and edges can go anywhere. So much so that it can be impossible to set a field to cover every eventuality.

Chris Gladwin It was a very disappointing season for a guy who started off in such good form. In his first season he scored over 1,000 runs in a very aggressive style, taking the bowlers on. Then he suffered a back injury which has obviously held up his progress a bit more than was thought. But maybe the thing which has caught up with him is the second year syndrome. I do think he has the natural ability to put this lean year behind him and make a name in the future. Maybe he could do with losing a bit of weight, that might help. And he could also become a little more dedicated to it. I think he is what you would term a lazy cricketer. He has got the talent but to make it at the top level, you must have not only talent but plenty of drive. If I had to be critical that is the area in which I would criticize him.

Brian Hardie Brian is a great example of a guy who has made the absolute most of what he has got. He is a tremendous team man, they don't come much better than him. It is a joy to play cricket with him in the team because he gets so much fun out of everything. He is a fantastic bloke and he never seems that upset with things. He is always very jovial on and off the field and yet he gets his runs in the bank. The runs scored during the summer played a considerable part in the team's success even though he was out for some time with a damaged finger. Brian takes every bowler and every attack as just another; he considers them all fair game to get his runs against. Bowlers will always find him frustrating but the sheer consistency of the guy over the course of a season, proves that talk of a lucky batsman isn't appropriate. Brian makes his own luck and if he seems to get away with snicks and edges at times, he is just as likely to play a classical cover drive for four in the same innings and some authentic pull shots.

Neil Foster Neil has a terrific attitude, he wants to work hard. His hundred wickets in the season was a terrific performance. Neil doesn't mind the responsibility he is given at Essex, like bowling fifteen overs on the trot sometimes. He enjoys taking wickets, a criterion for all successful bowlers. But against that, I would like to see him become a little bit tighter all round with what he does. He tends to have a good period for, say, two or three matches and then slacken off a little. But even during those two or three games, he can go through a session where he doesn't bowl that well, or he wastes the new ball. I think it is just work in the nets that is needed to solve that, analysing what you can and can't do. There is no point trying to do something which is not part of your make-up. It's all about working out what your limitations are and trying to operate within them. But his record this season shows that he ought to be a top-line international bowler for years to come. He will be even more effective too when he gains that consistency which experience tends to bring.

John Lever After Keith Fletcher, he is Mr Essex! He has been part of this cricket success story for the last ten years and Essex have got there on blokes like John, the ultimate workhorse. He gets the ball in his hand and you almost have to prise it out of his grasp. He loves taking wickets, doing well for Essex rather than just a personal thing. He never likes being taken off. But all that bowling, the wear and tear is bound to take its toll and he is experiencing a few problems from just that. But he is still capable of doing a great job. He is another player who doesn't get too upset with things. He does his job and some days he will get slogged, others he will take a lot of wickets. But you can bet he will always be in there trying 100%. You don't find that sort of character every day.

Alan Lilley Alan is a player I cannot quite work out, in terms of what the County expects of him or what he wants out of his career. He desperately wanted to get capped for years and that honour came at the end of this season. Maybe that will make a big difference to him next season, in terms of greater personal confidence and ability to earn a regular place in the side. I think he has been unfortunate in that he has been a naïve cricketer in a lot of ways.

He hasn't looked after No. 1, perhaps because he is so much an Essex team man. He will happily bat at No. 7 or 8 in a one-day game and go in looking for quick runs. Sometimes he will only make ten but in the context of a one-day match, that can be decisive. He is a brilliant fielder, worth his weight in gold at backward cover point or anywhere in the field. And Essex have done very well as a result of that type of cricketer who has been prepared to do all that and not grumble about it. But I believe he has suffered himself. I think if he were a little more ruthless in seeking to achieve his own personal goals, he would probably have been capped years ago. But perhaps you would have a lesser sort of player in terms of a team man. He played some really important innings for us, like the century at Jesmond and an eighty later in the summer. He made the runs when we needed them. So I would have to say I think he has been slightly mishandled in some areas.

I don't know the full picture because I can only go on what I have seen in this one summer. But certainly he deserved to be capped and I hope that launches him to greater things in the coming seasons.

Paul Prichard It is up to him now whether he breaks through into Test match cricket. Deep down, he is ruthless enough although outwardly, you wouldn't think so. I believe he doesn't like getting out at any time and he loves scoring a lot of runs. But he is an Essex personality and although they play the game the right way, it is a light-hearted approach at some stages so I don't know whether that will affect his chances of becoming an England player. He certainly has all the attributes to play Test match cricket. If he were a young player in Australia he might even be playing in Tests by now. I don't get the impression from Paul that he thinks he is ready to play for England yet. But that is up to him. But my view is that if they're good enough, get them into the Test scene whatever their age. If they have got the ability, they will show it. Paul could be one of those because to my mind he has the talent to play Test match cricket.

John Stephenson He is another good young cricketer. He and Prichard are about the same age, but you would think Prichard is much older. John should develop a lot more as he gets used to what it is being a first-class cricketer. He has got a lot of talent and is a very good competitor. He desperately wants to do well and has got all the right attributes but he might be a bit later in developing than a player like Prichard.

At the moment, John appears to me to be more of an accumulator rather than a strokemaker. But certainly when he does decide to play shots, for instance in one-day cricket, he will play all the strokes there are. He is a good striker of the ball, in fact, and perhaps just needs that extra confidence greater experience brings to go for shots all the time, in every sort of match.

Don Topley 'Toppers' is a funny sort of character. He is one of these guys that in every dressing room cops the brunt of the verbal abuse or the practical jokes. If something goes wrong, it is always blamed on him. If someone spills a drink, it is him. He is one of these sort of people and I suppose it adds to the atmosphere of the room. But there is no joke when he is out in the middle taking wickets – he looks a very good, competitive cricketer. If you put the ball in his hands, he never ever wants to come off. He will bowl all day if you want him to. He is going to be a very good cricketer for Essex. It was a good, shrewd move getting him from the ground staff at Lord's because even though you might look at his character as being one of those people you take the mickey out of, I think his performances this year have shown that he can bowl and bowl damn well. Given a couple of years at it, he will be a very handy cricketer indeed for Essex. He is a bit quicker than the Surrey bowler Graham Monkhouse, and he can bat a bit. He will get in there among the best of the bowlers and not be afraid to try his best. He has no fear, and he's got a responsible technique. He is confident and isn't worried about reputations, which I like to see in a young bowler.

Keith Pont People tell me that he joined the staff at the same time as Graham Gooch and was far and away a better cricketer at that time. Yet they are poles apart now. What happened in the meantime, I don't know. Whether Keith had the ultimate desire to do well at his cricket, I cannot say. But he has been part of the successful years and has done his job, and reasonably well too from what people say. He was the beneficiary this season and I was always happy to help him with anything I could. He is a nice guy, and a happy-go-lucky character. He is the one involved in the famous bicycle story. I don't know whether he was in the captain's bad books at the time but he was banished to fielding in the far outfield, at third man and fine leg. Somehow, the story goes, he got hold of this bicycle and was riding from one end of the ground to the other, going from third man to fine leg! Which was great amusement for everyone, apart from the captain, I imagine. But that is the sort of character he is and maybe that has been to his detriment as far as his cricket has been concerned. But that's the Essex style; some humour laced with the serious stuff. I enjoyed it – thanks for the memories, lads!

Derek Pringle Derek's season started all right but the ending will have disappointed him. He had a good opening for Essex, making runs and taking wickets. And he got into the England team and fitted in well. But as the summer wore on, so Derek's success slowed. He lost his England place and he didn't find taking wickets anything like so straightforward. I know he was greatly disappointed not to make the England party for the tour of Australia. It's hard to say just where he went off the rails and at which stage of the season. I had the feeling he wasn't moving the ball greatly, late in the summer. And I suppose that meant he didn't get so many wickets. All you can say is that he is potentially a high-class all-rounder. That's the view of many people and I subscribe to it. He has showed his worth in international cricket because he can bowl tightly and snap up the odd wicket here and there as well as making useful runs. Maybe his confidence suffered slightly, but I don't see why he shouldn't play for England again in the future. He has the ability and is always going to be a useful performer especially in English conditions.

Postscript

Essex clinched their fourth County Championship title in just eight years with two exciting victories in the run-in to the end of the season. By the time Alan Border had arrived home in Brisbane, Essex were already firmly emphasizing their superiority over their closest challengers for the title, Gloucestershire.

Poor 'Glos'; doomed forever, it would appear, to be the blushing bridesmaids, never the bride. It was to be the sixth time this century that the County of the famous Doctor, W. G. Grace, missed out on the Championship. Gloucestershire have still to register their first Championship title success in the 1900s.

The meeting of the summer's two outstanding Counties, in the Championship, was at Colchester on August 20, 21 and 22. Essex were without Border, of course, and Graham Gooch, the latter on Test match duty, so John Stephenson and Alan Lilley were brought in. But team spirit – that commodity Essex seem to have cornered the market in over recent years – nobly served the men of Southend and Chelmsford.

Essex, batting first, had a typically consistent first innings, which totalled 311; East 82, Prichard 65, Lilley 37, Fletcher 35, Hardie 26 and Foster 22. By the close on the first evening, two Gloucester-shire men had gone for 66; status quo.

The next day, Gloucestershire were spun a beautiful web by their former left-arm bowler, John Childs, who took eight for 58 in 22 overs. The wicket was turning, to be sure it was; Graveney had three Essex men by the close for 98, yet he could not deny the splendid East reaching stumps unbeaten on 55. On the final morning, East was to reach 100 not out as Essex declared at 172 for five, leaving Gloucestershire an exceedingly tricky 301 for victory on the wearing pitch. Victory was out of the question; survival was uppermost in the batsmen's minds. They made it, too, like thirsty men in the desert stumbling into the oasis at the eleventh hour. Gloucestershire were 139 for nine at the end, Childs finishing with the astonishing figures of 41–21–37–3. In fact, Essex bowled 91 overs in the second innings, making Gloucestershire's long struggle for survival agonizing in the extreme. The patient Bainbridge, with 53 not out, stood supreme so Essex were thwarted. Yet their maximum bonus points to Gloucestershire's five, closed the gap at the top still further; a relentless march of Gooch's men towards another title.

Rain ruined the County Championship game against Surrey at Chelmsford, washing out the final day and interrupting play for most of the match. However, Essex still secured vital points – five – to enhance their bag for the season.

Frustration at Chelmsford was to become joy away from the county, as Essex won their next two championship fixtures, to make virtually certain of the title. Yet when Essex, batting first at Taunton, were dismissed for 129, who would have thought the title was so close? Somerset, themselves in some strife at the end of an unpredictable first day at 134 for six, stretched their advantage by making 200 the next day, a lead of 71. Time, it seemed, for yet another of those famous Essex shows all the way down the order. The old faithfuls did not let their supporters down.

Gooch was lost, for 38, by the second evening; Prichard for the same score. But 213 for five (a lead of only 142) became 343 for seven next day as Hardie made a splendid, unbeaten 113. Typically, the lower order batsmen chipped in; Lever making 38 and East, batting at No. 8, a valuable 41. The declaration was challenging; Somerset were asked to score 272 in what proved to be 59 overs. A bad start; 38 for two. Then recovery to 100 for three. Another slip at 110 for four. Essex men fidgeted nervously in their seats beneath the Quantocks. Richards was the man; they had to get him. And suddenly Marks was with him, on 56, and Somerset were threatening to steal victory. At last, a breakthrough; Marks was gone. But who was this strutting onto the stage? Botham. Essex men repaired for refreshment. The situation demanded strong nerves (and strong ales).

At 253 for five with just 19 runs needed and the great men together, Essex were dead. Or at least an ordinary County would have been. And what happened in the next few minutes confirmed Essex's right to the title. Richards went for 94, Botham, 41. The last five wickets slid for just ten runs, Essex had won by nine runs and 20 points made them favourites for the first time in many weeks to take the title.

From Taunton to Folkestone, the championship roadshow rolled on. But there was an uncertain first innings batting display by Essex; Stephenson, Prichard, Hardie, East, Foster and Lever were all out for single figures. Conversely and most opportunely, Gooch made 74, Fletcher 47 and Pringle was 75 not out overnight at 252 for nine. The morning saw Pringle out within one shot of his 100, for a fine 97. But the weather was no friend, Kent spluttering to 177 for seven from 77 overs. Chris Cowdrey (who could ever forget his magnificent century on a brute of a pitch at Colchester in 1984) was 45 not out. Cowdrey finished the next day on 60, Kent closed 56 behind and Essex's declaration at 127 for three (Stephenson 71) asked Kent to score 183 to win. They had just over 50 overs in which to get the runs.

Benson and Taylor were worthy foes, Aslett too, but the middle order was as steady as a pack of cards out of balance. Kent declined from 47 without loss to 92 for six. Childs was their tormentor, taking seven for 58 in a total of 160 for match figures of ten for 123. A rich haul for Essex, 22 points. Now the title was just around the corner.

That title was clinched, irony of ironies, against the county which had broken Allan Border's dream of a Cup final appearance with Essex at Lord's – Nottinghamshire. Bonus points were enough for Essex at Trent Bridge and they duly arrived on the first day as Lever took five for 87 to help bowl out Notts for 267 and secure the all important point which won the title. Essex, 92 for two in reply by the close, must have had some night – they were all out for 139 the next morning! But a steadier second innings batting display (once the Champagne had cleared away) ensured the game was saved. Gooch, Fletcher, Lilley and East all made 40s and 232 for six, chasing 313, was enough for the draw.

The final Championship game was a rank anti-climax, Glamorgan winning at Chelmsford by 112 runs for only their second victory in the Championship all summer. A more unlikely outcome one could not have envisaged, especially after Glamorgan were 73 for six in their first innings! It was a rain interrupted match which the new Champions never came to terms with.

But success in the Championship was not to be followed with a win in the Sunday League. A surprise home defeat by Surrey at Chelmsford in August – Essex 163 for eight, Surrey 167 for nine – cost Essex the chance of a double. Yet, as Border himself felt all summer, the Championship was the true guide, the real barometer of a side's ability and quality. And in taking the Champions' title yet again, Essex had proved their right to be called the most successful and consistent County of the 1980s to date. They finished fourth in the Championship the previous season; now it was their turn to win the trophy once again.

In a season where Allan Border felt he never really showed his best form in front of the Essex supporters, and when players like Gooch, Lever, Pringle and Foster all played in Test matches, Essex's ability to emerge whatever the impediments to success had triumphed again. It had been merely the latest illustration of the worth, the proven value, of what Border called 'The Essex way'.

Appendix

Allan Border's playing record for Essex CCC in 1986

Date	Venue	Opponents	Competition	1st Inn.	2nd Inn.	Results
23 Apr–25 Apr	Fenner's	Camb. Univ.	F	80	—	D
26 Apr–28 Apr	Edgbaston	Warwicks	BAC	34	—	D
3 May	Hove	Sussex	B + H	11	—	W
4 May	Chelm'fd	Warwicks	JPSL	40	—	W
7 May–9 May	Chelm'fd	Kent	BAC	14	38	L
10 May	Taunton	Somerset	B + H	7	—	W
13 May	Chelm'fd	Glos	B + H	31	—	W
15 May	Chelm'fd	Glamorgan	B + H	17	—	W
18 May	Swindon	Glos	JPSL	12 no	—	W
21 May–23 May	Chelm'fd	Yorks	BAC	1	—	W
25 May	Sheffield	Yorks	JPSL	4	—	L
28 May	Chelm'fd	Notts	B + H (qf)	15	—	L
31 May–3 Jun	Derby	Derbys	BAC	110	—	W
1 Jun	Derby	Derbys	JPSL	10	—	W
4 Jun–6 Jun	Swansea	Glamorgan	BAC	150	—	W
7 Jun–10 Jun	Chelm'fd	Notts	BAC	13	50	D
8 Jun	Chelm'fd	Notts	JPSL	58	—	W
14 Jun–17 Jun	Ilford	Hants	BAC	71	54	L
15 Jun	Ilford	Hants	JPSL	75	—	L
18 Jun–20 Jun	Ilford	Sussex	BAC	17	96 no	W
21 Jun–24 Jun	Lord's	Middlesex	BAC	4	59 no	W
22 Jun	Lord's	Middlesex	JPSL	29	—	NR
25 Jun	Jesmond	Northumb	NW 1	23	—	W
2 Jul–4 Jun	Chelm'fd	New Zeal'd	T	4	14	L
5 Jul–8 Jul	Old Traff.	Lancs	BAC	6	51	L
6 Jul	Old Traff.	Lancs	JPSL	5	—	L
9 Jul	Edgbaston	Warwicks	NW 2	6	—	L
13 Jul	Chelm'fd	Somerset	JPSL	40	—	W
16 Jul–19 Jul	S'thend	Leics	BAC	45	12	L
19 Jul–22 Jul	S'thend	Worcs	BAC	56	13	W
20 Jul	S'thend	Worcs	JPSL	17	—	W
23 Jul–25 Jul	The Oval	Surrey	BAC	52	138	D
2 Aug–5 Aug	Eastb'ne	Sussex	BAC	2	108 no	D
3 Aug	Eastb'ne	Sussex	JPSL	2	—	W
6 Aug–8 Aug	Chelm'fd	Middlesex	BAC	45	—	W

9 Aug–12 Aug	Leicester	Leics	BAC	0	—	W
10 Aug	Leicester	Leics	JPSL	13	—	W
16 Aug–19 Aug	Colchester	Northants	BAC	28	6	L
17 Aug	Colchester	Northants	JPSL	25	—	W

Key

BAC	Britannic Assurance Championship	qf	quarter-final
B + H	Benson & Hedges Cup	no	not out
JPSL	John Player Sunday League	W	win
NW	NatWest Trophy	D	draw
F	Friendly match	L	loss
T	Tourist match	NR	no result

First Class Batting Average

Innings	32
Not outs	4
Runs	1385
Hundreds	4
Highest score	150
Average	49.46

Essex's record in 1986

Britannic County Championship

	P	W	L	D	Bt	Bl	Pts
Essex (4)	24	10	6	8	51	76	287
Glos (3)	24	9	3	12	50	65	259
Surrey (6)	24	8	6	10	54	80	248
Notts (8)	24	7	2	15	55	80	247
Worcs (5)	24	7	5	12	58	72	242
Hants (2)	24	7	4	13	54	69	235
Leics (16)	24	5	7	12	55	67	202
Kent (9)	24	5	7	12	42	75	197
Northants (10)	24	5	3	16	53	60	193
Yorks (11)	24	4	5	15	62	59	193
Derbys (13)	24	5	5	14	42	70	188
Middlesex (1)	24	4	9	11	47	65	176
Warwicks (15)	24	4	5	15	61	51	176
Sussex (7)	24	4	7	13	46	56	166
Lancs (14)	24	4	5	15	41	51	156
Somerset (17)	24	3	7	14	52	52	152
Glamorgan (12)	24	2	7	15	39	47	118

1985 positions in brackets

John Player Sunday League

	P	W	L	NR	T	Pts
Hants (3)	16	12	3	1	0	50
Essex (1)	16	11	4	1	0	46
Notts (12)	16	10	5	1	0	42
Sussex (2)	16	10	6	0	0	40
Northants (5)	16	9	5	2	0	40
Kent (10)	16	7	5	3	1	36
Somerset (10)	16	8	6	2	0	36
Yorks (6)	16	7	6	2	1	34
Derbys (4)	16	7	9	0	0	28
Middlesex (12)	16	5	7	3	1	28
Warwicks (6)	16	5	7	2	2	28
Glamorgan (14)	16	6	9	1	0	26
Lancs (14)	16	6	9	1	0	26
Surrey (17)	16	5	8	2	1	26
Leics (6)	16	5	10	1	0	22
Worcs (16)	16	5	11	0	0	20
Glos (6)	16	3	11	2	0	16

1985 positions in brackets

Benson & Hedges Cup

Lost to Nottinghamshire in quarter-finals

NatWest Trophy

Lost to Warwickshire in second round